What people are saying about …

THE TWENTY-PIECE SHUFFLE

"Greg Paul writes about personal experiences beyond the imagination of most of us. This book won't just challenge your thinking; it will deliver a punch to your emotional gut. And it is the kind of punch we believers need. Read it at your own risk."

Mark Sanborn, speaker and author of *The Fred Factor* and *You Don't Need a Title to Be a Leader*

"Nobody haunts the house of God more with those who are missing and must be there—the poor—than Greg Paul. His writing proves that being a great stylist doesn't mean any diminution of substance. The church is only a holy haunt when its members are being enriched every day by poverty-haunted lives. Love this book."

Leonard Sweet, author of *11* and *Soul Salsa* and professor at Drew University, George Fox University (sermons.com)

"*The Twenty-Piece Shuffle* dares to declare a profoundly human, theological reality—that not only are we all irrevocably connected, but also we need each other in order to become more truly human! With all his heart and his life, Greg declares that these mysteriously transforming relationships connect to our deepest heart's need. Greg's personal, experiential, gospel-based theology is refreshingly sound, while the gifts of his remarkable friends inspire the human, spiritual journey."

Sister Sue Mosteller, international coordinator of L'Arche and author of *My Brother, My Sister*; *Body Broken, Body Blessed*; and *Light Through the Crack*

"While lectures and sermons have their place, they often have a harsh edge because they can quickly become prescriptive and pragmatic. Stories, in contrast, are often more gentle and invite us to experience reality as it is. Greg Paul is a master storyteller, one who quietly expands our understanding of the gospel and kingdom values in a way that is both disarming and convicting."

Rod Wilson, president and professor of counseling and psychology at Regent College, Vancouver, Canada

"Brutally observant, painfully gracious, annoyingly perceptive, awkwardly patient. This is Greg Paul. His book is even worse!"

Drew Marshall, host of *The Drew Marshall Show*

"With stories lovingly told but with neither sentimentality nor sensationalism, Greg Paul invites us on a journey home toward God. And the guides for this journey are none other than those who have experienced homelessness in its most devastating and violent forms. Paul receives these stories as gifts, and exercises a caring and respectful stewardship of them. When a crack addict scores a twenty-dollar piece of crack he or she walks away from the dealer with what Paul calls 'the twenty-piece shuffle.' It is a walk towards a high that will dull the pain and is an attempt to achieve an experience that is unachievable. It is a walk away from home. In this book we discover that we are all walking 'the twenty-piece shuffle.'"

Brian J. Walsh, coauthor of *Beyond Homelessness: Christian Faith in a Culture of Dislocation* and Christian Reformed campus minister at the University of Toronto

"In *The Twenty-Piece Shuffle*, Greg Paul dips the nib of his most writerly pen into the recesses of his heart and tells us stories of redemption within pain and God's glory in the dirt. Paul's firsthand accounts of working with those in need in inner-city Toronto will break your heart. But his hope in God will knit it back together, hopefully in ways that will enable you to love as God loves and distribute that love to those who need it so desperately. In any case, *The Twenty-Piece Shuffle* helps us to see that in each destitute person resides the image of God, truly a human being just like you and me, and believe it or not, there's something we can learn from them. A beautiful book."

Lisa Samson, author of *Justice in the Burbs* and *Quaker Summer*

"Embedded in these supremely well-told stories of various encounters with the weird and wonderful is the deeply subversive message that we the middle class really need the poor and marginalized because they show us the depth of our own poverty. This book is just the kind of medicine that the missionally challenged Western church needs."

Alan Hirsch, author of *The Forgotten Ways* and *The Shaping of Things to Come* and cofounder of shapevine.com

"In Matthew's parable of the sheep and the goats, Jesus creates a startling scenario in which the world's losers become the judges of its winners. Jesus' upside-down kingdom aligns itself with the last, the lost, and the least and challenges his followers with the hard truth that we are all connected and that the quality of relationship that exists between the rich and the poor, between the "haves" and the "have-nots," is a defining measure of the authenticity of professed faith. *The Twenty-Piece Shuffle* fleshes out this idea in the context of Greg Paul's life and ministry in Toronto. It does so with the gentle graciousness and deft lyricism that is the hallmark of Greg's writing. Unlike every second film that Hollywood produces these days, *The Twenty-Piece Shuffle* is not based on a true story or even inspired by true events … it is both a true story and truth to boot."

Geoff Ryan, major in the Salvation Army, author of *Siren Call of a Dangerous God,* publisher of www.therubicon.org, and coordinator of the 614 network of urban communities

"It is a tall order to speak truth with both tenacity and warmth. It is an extraordinary feat to dig deep into true-life stories without exploiting those who've led them. And it is a profound gift to see God in all peoples, rich or poor, in a world that habitually designates souls into one of three categories: heroes, villains, or uneventful pedestrians. But Greg has led a life and found a voice that remarkably delivers 'the best of' on all counts. *The Twenty-Piece Shuffle* not only exposes why the poor and rich need each other—it erases the lines in the sand that categorize and divide them."

Tim Huff, author of *Bent Hope,* author and illustrator of *The Cardboard Shack Beneath the Bridge*, and director of Youth Unlimited, Toronto

"Greg unfolds the story of a sojourner's community wounded and scared by the gods of affluence and poverty. At Sanctuary the homeless, both poor and rich alike, have learned to journey well together, found safety in belonging, and discovered that each possesses wisdom to guide the other on the long road to home. A truly marvelous and insightful read. This is holy ground."

Rick Tobias, CEO of Yonge Street Mission, Toronto

THE TWENTY-PIECE SHUFFLE

WHY THE POOR AND RICH
NEED EACH OTHER

GREG PAUL

David C Cook®
transforming lives together

Published by David C. Cook
4050 Lee Vance View
Colorado Springs, CO 80918 U.S.A.

David C. Cook Distribution Canada
55 Woodslee Avenue, Paris, Ontario, Canada N3L 3E5

David C. Cook U.K., Kingsway Communications
Eastbourne, East Sussex BN23 6NT, England

The Web site addresses recommended throughout this book are offered as a resource
to you. These Web sites are not intended in any way to be or imply an endorse-
ment on the part of David C. Cook, nor do we vouch for their content.

All Scripture quotations, unless otherwise noted, are taken from the *Holy Bible, New International
Version®*. *NIV®*. Copyright © 1973, 1978, 1984 by International Bible Society. Used by permission
of Zondervan. All rights reserved. Scripture quotations marked KJV are from the King James Version
of the Bible. (Public Domain); and ESV are taken from *The Holy Bible, English Standard Version.*
Copyright © 2000; 2001 by Crossway Bibles, a division of Good News Publishers. Used by permission. All rights reserved. Italics in Scripture quotations have been added by the author for emphasis.

LCCN 2008929269
ISBN 978-1-4347-9942-5

The Team: Andrea Christian, Amy Kiechlin, Jack Campbell, and Karen Athen
Cover Design: Disciple Design, David Terry
Interior Design: Disciple Design
Cover Photo: Phillip Parker

Printed in the United States of America
First Edition 2008

1 2 3 4 5 6 7 8 9 10

052908

For the prophets of the parks, streets, alleys, and stairwells

CONTENTS

Acknowledgments   11

Chapter 1: The Long Road Home   13

Chapter 2: Defining "Home"   23

Chapter 3: Doing the Twenty-Piece Shuffle   27

Chapter 4: Guides for the Journey   35

Chapter 5: On the Way   45

The First Leg of the Journey
From Isolation to Intimacy   *51*

Chapter 6: Intimacy and Isolation   61

Chapter 7: From Independence to Communion   69

Chapter 8: From Impregnability to Vulnerability   83

The Second Leg of the Journey
From Productivity to Fruitfulness   *101*

Chapter 9: Productivity and Fruitfulness   113

Chapter 10: From Accomplishment to Essence   123

Chapter 11: From Wandering to Journeying   139

The Third Leg of the Journey
From Suffering to Glory   *155*

Chapter 12: Suffering and Glory   169

Chapter 13: From Anger to Sorrow   179

Chapter 14: From Death to Resurrection   193

Chapter 15: Arrival   213

Appendix   221

Notes   235

ACKNOWLEDGMENTS

It seems odd to me that a book like this, which on the surface is the product of the efforts of one person working in (usually) rigid solitude, is actually the fruit of at least dozens and probably hundreds of lives lived in messy, complicated, but ultimately fecund community. When I was a boy, I had a paper route, delivering to twenty-odd homes a daily compilation of stories from around the globe—a tiny, erratic sampling of the unknowable breadth of human drama. I feel that my role is much the same now: I deliver a narrow slice of the costly wisdom, the prophetic utterances and actions of my people. It's humbling and a great honor to do so.

So, first and foremost, all the people mentioned herein, whether by their real or assigned names, plus the whole Sanctuary community, including staff, board, worshippers, a slew of people who would usually be described as volunteers but for whom I prefer the more exalted, godly term "servants," hundreds of community members who live courageous lives amid deep darkness, partners who give generously of their money, time, and other resources—all these must be acknowledged as the true authors of what I am privileged to "deliver."

I'm grateful, too, for the inspiration and support offered by colleagues across the nation who are also engaged in seeking justice for people who are poor or excluded. These include people of many faiths (or none). Most particularly, my brothers and sisters who are part of StreetLevel, a national roundtable on poverty and homelessness (www.streetlevel.ca), are a source of constant encouragement.

Miller and Terri Alloway, of the Maranatha Foundation, provided both the time and the space (very beautiful space!) in which the greatest part of this book was written. It's anybody's guess if or when it would have been finished otherwise. Tim Huff shared that experience with me while working on a book of his own—it made a huge difference having such an encouraging, compatible writing buddy in the next room and with whom to hash over the day's work in the evening.

Don Pape, friend and publisher, championed this book from the start, as he did with *God in the Alley.* Andrea Christian, my editor, made it better and more concise.

Finally, my sons and daughter (Caleb, Jesse, Rachel, and Kelly), have, in ways that they won't begin to intuit until long after they've started having kids themselves, held me and kept me grounded during the difficult period in which this book was conceived. They're incredible people.

CHAPTER 1

THE LONG ROAD HOME

But trailing clouds of glory do we come
From God, who is our home....
—Wm. Wordsworth

I have to admit, I never liked Hanson[1] much anyway, but I cared for him even less when he walked into a Sanctuary drop-in one perfect June morning and remarked, "Somebody better go check on Arthur. He's squirming around on the grass outside, and he says he's gonna die."

A few months ago, I'd had to escort Hanson out of the building and inform him that he'd be barred for a month or so. Our rules are few and simple. I don't recall what the infraction was—knowing Hanson, it likely had to do with him beating or threatening to kill somebody— maybe both. Hanson was a big, handsome Ojibwa guy with a broad chest, long black hair, and a picturesque scar at the side of his mouth. He was a bully and a poser who threatened people he knew couldn't or wouldn't respond. Once in while, I'd find myself daydreaming about going toe-to-toe with him. It's a good thing my Christian principles kept me from following up. He'd have wiped the floor with me.

The day I ejected Hanson, he had been drinking mouthwash or rubbing alcohol, and he was raving. When I told him he'd have to go, I stood in front of him with my arms out wide so he couldn't go after whoever it was he had threatened (and so he'd know I wasn't threatening him). He stepped up to me so we were chest to chest and bumped me a couple of times, like baseball managers do to umpires when they want the folks in the bleachers to know they're sticking up for the team. His eyeballs were vibrating—yes, vibrating, as if he were a sugar-jacked ten-year-old with a new video game—and he was foaming at the mouth. He spit in my face once and took a little step back, waiting, I'm sure, for me to take a swing at him. I stepped right up close to him again, arms still sticking straight out to the sides, waiting for him to take a swing at me or head-butt me or, worse, ram his knee into my crotch; but he backed up. I stepped forward, we gained some kind of modest momentum, and in this herky-jerky two-step, I backed him up the length of the drop-in room, up the stairs, and out the front door. He threatened me, snarling and spewing all the way, but never laid a hand on me.

Other people in the drop-in, particularly those who knew Hanson from the street, said the situation was virtually miraculous. Hanson, I think, was a little disconcerted. I was just plain grateful. After that, he treated me pretty well—at least when he was sober. When he was drunk, it was another matter.

The day Hanson came in and announced Arthur was dying, he seemed to be sober. I didn't doubt there was something seriously wrong, but Hanson's nonchalance and unwillingness to do anything about it himself bugged me—after all, Arthur was his older brother. I called for Keren Elumir, our parish nurse at the time, and the two of us rushed outside.

Sanctuary is housed in a little old brown brick church building at the north end of Toronto's downtown core and just a stone's throw from Yonge Street, the city's traditional "Main Street." We don't have much space. Almost the whole front yard is covered with paving brick, and with some careful planning, we can squeeze as many as eight compact cars onto it. The grass Hanson had said Arthur was squirming on was (still is) really a small patch of hard-packed dirt with a few hardy blades poking through a fulsome crop of cigarette butts.

And sure enough, there's Arthur on his back amid the butts, with his head thrown back and his knees drawn up to his chest. Skinny, filthy fingers clutch his shins as he rocks back and forth, moaning. The cuffs of his jeans are frayed, and the legs are torn and dotted with cigarette burns. The rocking and moaning stop abruptly. His back arches, head lurches forward.

"I'm gonna die, I'm gonna die, I'm gonna die."

Keren kneels, lifts his head gently, and places it on her knees. She is trying to keep him from choking on his tongue or vomit. His eyes roll wildly up at her, disappearing momentarily behind the lids as if, once they're started in a given direction, he can't stop them. The pupils flutter back down into view, although they continue to dance and jerk around. His face twists and twitches. It is an ugly face—its nose poorly placed, the wrong size and shape, a wrinkled forehead, a wide, crooked mouthful of rotten teeth. The hair spread on Keren's lap is a mess of greasy black string, laced with monster flakes of dandruff that have come adrift of the islands of angry red psoriasis that dot his scalp. She gently pushes the hair away from his forehead and pats the sweat away with a wad of Kleenex.

"911?" I ask and, getting the nod, dial the number on my cell phone. Once I have navigated past the initial questions, I hand the phone over to her. Keren speaks calmly into the receiver and gently strokes Arthur's head each time he is hit with a spasm.

"S'wrong with him?" asks a street guy who has just arrived for the meal that is about to be served at Sanctuary. "Food poisoning?"

"Nope," says another voice. Turning, I realize Hanson has joined the handful of silent gawkers and is standing to the side at a respectful distance. His hands are folded in front of him as if facing a judge. "Arthur is dying now—from drinking the rubby."

Rubbing alcohol is what he means, or mouthwash, and he may be right. I kneel beside Arthur. Keren is relaying symptoms to the emergency operator as though dictating a particularly fussy recipe to a friend.

Arthur may be ugly, but he's a good guy—as decent as Hanson is nasty. Booze and street life have hollowed him out. His chest, almost covered by a ragged checked shirt crusted with what looks like dried excrement and blood and puke, threatens to cave in on itself. There seems to be no particular rhythm to its rise and fall. His arms are spindly, spotted with small scabs amid the blurry green jailhouse tattoos. The fingers that release their desperate grip on his shins to clutch his stomach every thirty seconds or so are discolored and split at the tips, like grapes gone bad.

"Hang on there, old-timer, the medics are coming."

A deep *unnnh!*, another rolling spasm, and his eyes veer away from me again. It sure looks to me like alcohol poisoning, which I imagine could kill him, given that Arthur's liver must be about the size and absorbency of a golf ball after the years of drinking. His brother

Al died, just a couple of winters ago, stoned on cough medicine: a couple of quiet seizures in the middle of the night, while packed head to toe with a bunch of other men in a shelter. A week or two before he passed, Al had posed in the basement at Sanctuary to have his silhouette painted on the wall. He stood with his head cocked and hands raised, half reaching, half supplicating. He was asking the Great Spirit to receive his soul, he had joked, to carry him away from this hell.

Suddenly, I am pierced with sorrow for Hanson, still standing in quiet, impassive reverence, watching his brother's withered body and soul being wrenched apart. Two older brothers gone or going. He can't help but think that the prophecy of his own future is being played out before him. He stood exactly this way, at the back of the Sanctuary auditorium, throughout Al's memorial. At the time, his lack of emotion seemed callous to me. Now it seems impossibly courageous.

"Arthur." I place a hand on his weak chest and bend over his face, which is now the greenish hue of a tornado sky. "Arthur. The ambulance is on its way. Do you want me to pray for you?"

I know this is risky—most of my aboriginal friends have good reason to be, at the very least, suspicious of anything Christian. But most also have a strong sense of connection to the Creator. Arthur squeezes out a painful but definite "uh-huh."

So I pray. Platitudes, mostly. Imploring the Creator to be with his child Arthur now in the midst of his pain and fear. To take that precious life in his hands. To protect his spirit. To be with Arthur in a way that he will know and feel, in a way that will grant him peace.

Although I believe that God is always close enough to touch, he never feels very near to me at times like this. And though I have known such prayers of mine to be, once in a while, comforting to the one being prayed for, to me in the moment they seem most often like empty, faintly silly words. Mostly they remind me of how completely helpless I am in any situation that really matters—and that, I suppose in my better moments, is the point.

The ambulance arrives with a skirl of sirens. One paramedic steps quickly from the cab, assesses the situation and the crowd of street people that has gathered, and turns back to get his gear. Two people appear, masked and gloved, and begin ordering people to stand back. Hanson is slow to move and receives a rude bark and a peremptory shove. He stumbles a bit but regains his balance and steps back, never taking his eyes from Arthur. Keren tries to brief the paramedics, but they aren't listening, and they clearly think the two of us should move away from Arthur too. Keren brushes the hair from Arthur's forehead and stays put.

I begin to stand up, but Arthur's eyes suddenly lock on mine.

"It took me two hours to get here," he says, clear as a bell. I nod and stand up.

Within minutes, the paramedics have bundled him onto a gurney and stashed him in the back of the ambulance. They motor off, no siren, without a backward glance. The crowd drifts off. Hanson is gone already. I catch a glimpse of him half a block away, turning onto Yonge Street, his black hair covering his proud shoulders.

I doubt that Arthur really remembers the event I've described here; he had so many others like it. For a few years, I expected almost weekly that I would hear that Arthur had finally died, but he's outlived several who seemed sturdier, less entrenched in the patterns of self-destruction. These days, when I ask his old street brothers how he's doing, they say simply, "Arthur's doing good," and change the subject. Arthur is sober and healthy, working for a center that provides services to the city's aboriginal street community. They keep their distance from Arthur, and he from them. This is the painful price of his sobriety. Although they honor it, they can't afford to look at it too closely.

$ $ $

It was only later that I thought about Arthur's "final" words to me. He and I both thought it was the last thing he'd ever say to me, and getting back to Sanctuary took everything he had. But what did it look like?

I imagine it like this:

Arthur wakes up in an alley somewhere. He is huddled in a doorway on a piece of soggy cardboard—he's pissed himself again—and his legs are tangled with those of one of his street brothers. Kevin, say. He can taste the bile in his throat, smells it in his hair, and thinks groggily, *Whoa! Lucky I was lyin' on my side.*

He lies there, looking at the empty Listerine bottles, remembers talking with Kevin about fishing back on the rez as they drank, but isn't sure who passed out first. He wonders why he's even awake, since the sun has not yet risen high enough to peek over the buildings.

A wave of pain rips through his stomach—the same pain that hunted him in his dreamless sleep and dragged him groaning into consciousness. He yelps and curses and wraps his arms around his stomach. The pain subsides slowly.

"What was that?" he croaks to himself.

Seizures he's had before. They're scary because you're so helpless, but they don't hurt like this. The thought is hardly complete when the pain attacks again, like an angry raccoon trapped inside his stomach. He kicks his legs free of Kevin's, wondering if they drank poison somehow and if Kevin is already gone. He struggles to his feet as quickly as he can, pushing his back against the brick behind him, and walking his shoulder blades up the wall.

"Kevin!" he shouts, but hears only a dry whisper. He boots the other man in the thigh, barely nudging him the first time, hard enough on the second try that Kevin rolls a bit. Enough to see that he's still breathing. He calls again, sure that he'll have another attack momentarily, but Kevin is comatose.

The pain returns and gets worse. Wave after wave, until there are no more waves, just one massive tidal rush of pain. He knows then that this is how he will die—here in this alley, amid fast-food containers and syringes. He has waited since he was a boy among drunken, dying adults for this drunken death to find him. He is only mildly surprised that it has appeared so soon: an invited guest who appears half an hour before the party is supposed to start.

But he will not die in this alley, he tells himself, hidden from the world and the sun, a human pile lost among the Dumpsters and stacks of plastic milk crates. The end of the alleyway seems far off. He does not yet know where he is going but trusts his spirit will lead him. He pulls himself along the length of a car, grabbing the door handles. He shuffles feet of stone through a cluster of used condoms, dry and wrinkled brown like shucked skin.

"Whoa!" he wheezes out loud. "Must be the Sacred Penis Burial Ground here." He laughs to himself but pays for it immediately.

Out of the alley, the sun is blinding, a white light that washes the people and buildings thin. He has no sense of where he is. Nothing looks familiar; nothing makes sense. Everything he sees appears to him as a bad collage of mismatched elements. Somewhere high up, a flashing message: 9:13, and a second later, 26°C. Strange faces looming in and out of view. Distant voices asking something unintelligible.

At one point, Arthur realizes he is curled up in a doorway and wonders if he has actually moved at all, but Kevin is not here, the sun is bright, the sound of traffic is only a few feet away. An ugly white woman holds her face a foot away from his, yammering some nonsense at him. After she goes away, he tries to clamber to his feet again, but the pain in his stomach has commandeered all his strength. His legs fold up, knees to his chest, under a power that seems to come from somewhere beyond his body. Some time later he finds he is up and staggering, bouncing off shop windows—Yonge Street?—but has no idea how this came about. It's as if this pain were a thick fog obscuring everything but an occasional and random sight or sound.

When it parts next, he sees his feet, at a great distance, shuffling along below him over reddish paving brick that is oddly familiar. There are faces, too, that he recognizes: street faces, not suits or shopgirls. They are smoking, looking at him but saying nothing. Beyond them is an arched limestone doorway, battered plank doors propped wide open. And he understands, then, where his spirit has led him.

He wants to mount the three steps to the doorway but finds he can't lift his feet far enough. Ah well. He has come far enough; this is close enough. His legs collapse, and he settles on a bed of hard-packed dirt and cigarette butts. Another spasm yanks his knees up to his chest.

A pair of formerly white cross-trainers stops beside him.

"Arthur? What's wrong with you?"

Arthur never liked Hanson much, although you're really not supposed to admit that about your own brother. Too proud, too disrespectful. Hanson is too strong now, too, Arthur admits to himself, thinking of the many nasty things he did to Hanson as a child and how weak he himself has become.

"I'm gonna die," he says, and saying it out loud sets free a fear that rides his pain like a boy on a wild horse. This is the place. He is terrified, but he is safe. He is finally home.

CHAPTER 2

DEFINING "HOME"

The home should be the treasure chest of living.
—Le Corbusier, recalled upon his death

Arthur's journey from alley to Sanctuary is, as I've related it, only what I have imagined, but it can't be far from what really happened. He woke up somewhere that morning in great pain, became convinced he was about to die, and spent the next two hours staggering his way to our front door.

"Imagine what I've been through just to find my way here, just to lie in this dirt with my head in Keren's lap and your hand on my heart," he said to me. It was only in imagining what the journey cost him that I came to realize how important it was and why he wanted me to know that it was important.

Because if you're in pain, you want to be welcomed, comforted, cared for.

Because if you're dying, you want to be somewhere safe enough to fight it or to let go.

Because when you're out in the big bad world and things go terribly wrong, or wonderfully right, you want to go home. To mourn or to celebrate. To not have to be strong or reserved anymore—to give in to the need to tremble with fear, or be giddy with joy. To be able to do all of that without being humiliated or alone.

Because when you're not welcome anywhere else, home, as Robert Frost wrote, is where, when you go there, they have to take you in. You can really live there—grow, dream, create. For a child growing up in a healthy, loving home, anything seems possible.

I have always had some version of a healthy home. I grew up in a Christian family with two brothers and a father and mother who loved me and still do. We were wealthier and more privileged in every way than I could comprehend at the time. Karen and I married when I was twenty-two, and we started our own home. Ten years later, I also had four kids and a house of my own (although, to this day, the bank owns a substantial chunk of it). My children are older now, and two live elsewhere, but they still come home often. And although our marriage staggered through a number of difficult years to a painful conclusion in 2006—a wrenching negation of "home" that was the bitterest experience of my life—we had years of mostly peace and stability that are still a precious foundation for who and what I am now.

I had a church "home" where I was appreciated and supported—so much so that the congregation and leadership commissioned Karen and me as missionaries to the downtown core of Toronto. They trusted me enough to let me root that ministry in playing rock 'n' roll in smoky bars. And now, years later, many of the people of Richvale Bible Chapel still support the ministry that became Sanctuary to a degree that is humbling.

Sanctuary is home to me in so many ways. Although many in the community refer to me as the pastor of the Sanctuary church, I go on Sundays to be fed—and I am, without fail! This, I think, is a rarity for leaders in conventional churches. Our drop-ins, and the streets, alleys, bars, and coffee shops of the neighborhood are as familiar to me

as my own bedroom; I am surrounded by friends, some of whom feel
almost like family to me. I can hardly walk a block from Sanctuary's
front doors without someone calling my name, bumping fists, asking,
"How's it goin'?" (Or, "Got a quarter?") My "colleagues" on staff are
true brothers and sisters.

The band, Red Rain, has been a kind of home too. Since 1985,
I've practiced, performed, and prayed with Dan, Les, and (since '94)
Doug. In '06, Phil arrived, bringing the big fat gorgeous sound of his
Hammond B3 organ with him. We've been through all kinds of deep
water together. No doubt we're headed for more. We've played together
in many dark places, but we've also had the best seats in the house at
some gloriously wild celebrations.

I have been profoundly and richly blessed with "home."

But it's never enough—I always hunger for more.

Actual material homelessness is a rising problem in the Western
world. In some cities homeless people are policed into one area, and
in others they are policed into hiding, but it is never difficult to find
the mysterious figures with tatty beards and haunted eyes, wearing
multiple layers of ragged clothing and huddling beneath bridges, in
doorways, on subway grates, around fires lit in steel drums, in lean-tos
of cardboard and plastic sheeting. Men prematurely old. Young girls
who know too much too soon. The flotsam and jetsam of the wealthiest society the world has ever known.

These are the people who are at the heart of the Sanctuary
community—men and women and transgendered people who struggle with addiction, mental illness, traumatic histories, and present
circumstances that are an impossible mix of poverty, violence, con-
tinual danger, exclusion, systemic oppression, abusive sex, and more.

Even those who have a roof over their heads, often in rooming houses that plumb the depths of the term "grim," are, in the most essential way, homeless. They have never experienced the kind of warm embrace summed up in that simple word "home." Where they should have been nurtured, they endured violence; the very relationships that ought to have taught them to trust were characterized by betrayal of the meanest sort.

Is it any wonder, then, that most people in most places view my homeless brothers and sisters as "them"—burdens on society, hopeless, perhaps dangerous? But how can "they" display respect for themselves or others when they have been raised on a diet of contempt? Some Christians might say, with that peculiar mixture of smugness and relieved resignation, "The poor you will always have with you."[1]

I have so much to learn from my homeless friends. They teach me how much I take for granted and how sweet and rare safety and a true welcome are. My friends who have been outcasts all their lives because of mental illness reveal how deeply I still long to know that I really matter, that I am precious. My friends who struggle with addiction show me how rapacious my hunger is for ecstasy, for fulfillment—in a word, for glory.

My life, as blessed as I am, is filled with longing, pierced by a hunger that has never truly been sated. I'm like the prodigal, adrift and ravenous in a distant land, disappointed by most of what I have so eagerly sought, often disappointed with myself. My every experience of "home" has been fractured, ephemeral: scraps of rich meat thickly marbled with the indigestible gristle of failure, disillusionment, and broken relationship.

Like Arthur, I want to find a way home.

CHAPTER 3

DOING THE TWENTY-PIECE SHUFFLE

Hunger is insolent, and will be fed.
—*Homer,* **The Odyssey**

I recognized Benny from behind and halfway across the drop-in room. I don't know how, given that it had been ten years since I had seen him last. He had lost that hungry, skulking look—lost a little hair too, but gained weight and a certain presence. I called his name. As he turned toward me, I could see that the pounds filling out the tight white T-shirt were mostly muscle.

"Well, look at you!" he said, stepping forward to shake my hand. "You look like you joined the marines."

It might have been the khaki tank top I was wearing, but it was probably, I thought ruefully, the hair, which used to be brown and shoulder length, but was, by now, reduced to gray stubble.

"Benny, you scamp!" I had said, ten years earlier, when I heard his voice over the phone. "I saw you in the papers, man. You been doing banks in my neighborhood! The Scotiabank at Pape and Danforth is my branch—if you do that one too, I'll have to hunt you down myself!"

He had laughed; a giddy, happy kind of laugh. "You can relax, bud. They caught me already."

His phone call had been a surprise. For an uncomfortable moment I had thought that he was still on the run and looking to me for some form of help that I wouldn't be able to give, but he was just calling to say hi. He had no one else to call, I guess.

Benny had originally been sent away on an assortment of small-time beefs—simple assault, shoplifting, b & e, the inevitable "failure to appear"—and was weeks from being released when he and a buddy decided they'd had enough and escaped from the minimum security facility. They stole a jail guard's car, then held up a gas station for fuel, cigarettes, pop, and chips, before booting it straight back to Toronto.

Once back in the city it took him no time at all to boost a couple of defused hand grenades from an army surplus store. He and his running mate knew it was probably a matter of days before they got nailed by the cops. They determined they'd go back to the joint with some status and have some fun in the meantime.

Over the phone, he'd told me they had held up a dozen banks in less than a month with those bogus grenades, netting more than a hundred grand, and never bothered to cover their faces or even wear hats for the cameras. When I asked, half-serious, where they had stashed the money, he claimed they had spent every dollar. They were broke when they woke up in a room at the Sheraton at four o'clock in the morning, in the center of a pool of light cast by a dozen flashlights mounted on police assault rifles.

"Ooo-ee!" Benny crowed down the phone line. "*That* was an adrenaline rush!"

"So when are you in court next?" I asked, thinking of the usual round of five or six appearances necessary to get to an actual trial.

"Oh, I pled already. Got another fourteen years."

I didn't know anything about Benny's early life, but he'd lived on the street for a long time. Years of being a hungry skinny kid, at the wrong end of every deal, an easy target for anyone with a few bucks and a closet full of bizarre sexual tastes. Running with a pack of other kids like him—bold, brilliant young improvisers in whom every reasonable fear or physical boundary had long since been eradicated. Periodically one of them would, by some miracle, gain free access to an apartment that was vacant or unattended; within hours, a dozen or more would gather and set up camp. They slept wherever they fell; defecated in the nearest corner if the washroom was occupied; coupled frequently, randomly, without regard to gender, relationship, or the number of participants. Half-full fast-food containers piled up; mice gathered. It never lasted more than a week or two—nobody ever expected it to—and the whole group would be back out on the street again, running, hustling, having fistfights over slights real and imagined. The whole insane dance was fueled by a voracious hunger for crack cocaine.

Sanctuary was one of this group's very few regular places during that period. They ate like animals, passed out on the couches, received fresh socks and underwear, and left their filthy old ones on the floor of the washroom. One time Benny and his girlfriend PJ hid under a pile of clothing in the storage room and fell asleep, setting off the security alarm when they woke up in the middle of the night and tried to find their way out of the darkened building. They were irritating, vulgar, demanding, selfish—and touchingly beautiful, as teenagers often are.

I remembered Benny and PJ sprawled together on a couch planted squarely in front of the stage on a night when Red Rain, the Sanctuary house band, was releasing its first CD. They stayed the whole evening, listening intently.

"Hey," said Benny, sidling up to me at the end of the concert. "You know that one song you did?"

We had done a couple of dozen, but I knew immediately which song he was referring to: "Boystown," a song about the dark streets not far from Sanctuary where boys and young men prostitute themselves to survive. I nodded.

"That's about us, isn't it?" Eyes brimming bright. "That's why you go walking around out there at night, isn't it? So you'll know? And you're playing the song so people will know about us." He looked around to see if anyone was listening in.

"You know that long white limousine?" he said, referencing a line from the song: *a long white limousine / come cruising like a shark.*[1] "Well, I been in it."

All things considered, why wouldn't Benny want to go back to jail? Three hots and a cot, as they say. Order, cleanliness, warmth, clothing, stability. With his new status as an armed bank robber with multiple offenses, he'd be very near the top of the heap in the jailhouse social ranking—certainly much, much higher than he had been in any society before. For a guy who had never planned anything more than three or four hours in advance, the fourteen-year sentence was simply a guarantee that the most comfortable, secure situation he had ever known would be his for a virtual eternity. It would be a home of sorts.

And now here he was a decade later, out on parole, with a chaperone from the halfway house grinning self-consciously at his elbow, asking if he could volunteer at Sanctuary. Sure he could, but would our drop-ins be a safe place for him? He smiled tightly. He knew what I meant.

"Yeah, I don't do that s*** no more. I been clean a long time."

He looked it. He sounded like it. No jubilance at being out; a measured wariness, the quiet confidence of a man who has nothing he needs to prove. We talked a little, just superficial stuff. An old street connection recognized him too. It wasn't someone he'd known well, and Benny didn't welcome him with any joy, but he joined the conversation anyway. Benny said he had to go—that he would call to sort out volunteering details.

We said good-bye. He headed for the door, trailing his halfway house buddy and the street guy, who scampered along at his shoulder, saying something in low, urgent tones into Benny's ear. Benny stopped. The guy bumped into him, backed up as Benny turned.

"Leave me alone," Benny said. Not loudly, but very clearly. Nailing him with a calm, direct stare. "I don't do that s*** no more." The guy peeled hastily away.

We don't, as a matter of policy, allow people to carry drugs, alcohol, or weapons into our drop-ins, let alone deal, share, or use them; but we don't strip-search people either, so we know it happens some anyway. *Still*, I thought, *how bad is that*? Benny comes back after all this time to offer his help, and the only one in the place who even recognizes him apart from me is some jerk whose first thought is that Benny might be in a position to buy or sell some rock. His measured response impressed me. I remembered how it used to be with him.

It seems to me it was a cool, bright September day, but I could be mistaken. It was a long time ago. I'm sure, though, that it wasn't warm enough that you would naturally perspire. I was coming back from a jaunt somewhere down Yonge Street and bumped into Benny in the middle of the parking lot that used to be beside Sanctuary. It's part of a chain of parkettes now, just a half a block east of Yonge Street. This pleasant little corridor of green allows local apartment-dwelling dogs attended by their acolytes a place to dump and is a respite from concrete and glass. Back then it was a broken sheet of glass-strewn asphalt, a simple corral for a hundred or so of the city's herd of restless automobiles.

Benny and I stood there, chatting about nothing in particular, just a stone's throw from the Charles Street end of the parking lot. He was looking over my shoulder, absently watching cars and pedestrians droning by, looking tired and pale.

I saw his eyes lock on to something, a car passing, and follow it down the street. His pale skin turned instantly gray, the sweat jumped from his forehead, and his whole body started to shake. I turned in time to see the object of his attention, a battered subcompact, make the turn and disappear onto Yonge Street. I had never seen such an obvious and instantaneous physical reaction to a purely visual stimulation, so I asked him about it.

The car belonged to his crack dealer. Merely seeing it pass had set him to jonesing in a heartbeat.

The evil genius of crack is that it's cheap, fast, and has few direct aftereffects. The basic unit of sale is a twenty-dollar piece of chalky white crystal—a "twenty-piece"—that's good for about four quick blasts, if you're smoking it. (It can be dissolved and injected too, which is a whole other story.) It's just enough to share with one other person, maybe your street partner, or maybe somebody you're trying to buy off or buy up one way or another. You go up like a rocket, down like a stone, and you're ready to race again in a matter of minutes.

The high is so intense that some people claim to become addicted after just one use. It's certainly not uncommon in our community for people to go on runs that last several days at a time, during which they forgo food, sleep, and most other forms of comfort, locked into a grueling round of *get money, score drugs, do drugs; get money, score drugs, do drugs* ...

Benny excused himself abruptly and hustled off toward Yonge Street. I strolled off in the other direction. Minutes later and a few blocks away, I saw him across the street. He was perky now, jaunty even, elbows cocked and swinging, head up and straight ahead like he was locked on a target, rolling heel to toe in a brisk, excited walk. He was preoccupied, as if there was somewhere he just had to be as soon as humanly possible. One hand was clenched tight, and I knew within that fist was a square of paper folded around a chalky white crystal.

We have a name around here for that particular way of walking. We call it "The Twenty-Piece Shuffle."

CHAPTER 4

GUIDES FOR THE JOURNEY

I have the desire to do what is good, but I cannot carry it out.
For what I do is not the good I want to do; no, the evil I do not
want to do—this I keep on doing.... What a wretched man I am!
Who will rescue me from this body of death?
—Paul, Romans 7:18–19, 24

Is there a quote anywhere in Paul's writing that is easier to relate to than the one above?

Benny and I come from very different early life experiences—I don't know much about his, but I can only imagine what home life was like if hustling on the street seemed like a better deal. Our circumstances throughout the course of our relationship haven't exactly been parallel either. In fact, I haven't seen him again since he dropped by that last time. Maybe he concluded our environment was too dangerous for him after all. Still, he and other friends from the street have become guides on my journey. The very extremity of their lives helps pull the lid off the containers where I tend to stuff my own desires. And I know, if only because he came back after ten years, that friends like Benny also find some value in walking with me. Despite many detours, blind alleys, broken roads, and seemingly impassable paths, we—the wild variety of pilgrims in our community (addicts, professional people, university students, people who struggle with mental illness, some who live under bridges, and others who live in beautiful suburban houses), together, I believe, with the Spirit himself—are guiding each other home.

It used to be that when I saw one of my friends doing the twenty-piece shuffle, I shook my head in bemused wonder. Now I nod in recognition of its essential likeness to that eagerness with which I anticipate and chase after the things that I hope will grant me pleasure, peace, comfort ... even just a momentary relief from the deadly dullness that sometimes sucks the color from my days.

Benny used to give almost all his time and energy to arriving at that brief moment of euphoria; it could have cost him his life, and for more than a few friends I have had, it actually has. For my part, I don't seek that kind of blow-the-top-off-your-head excitement, and I parcel out my personal resources more carefully. The "drug" I crave is usually apparently more benign. It may even be the kind of thing the world around me heartily approves of: material goods, recognition for the work I do, upward mobility, security, proximity to people who are attractive or important, comfort, happiness. I mask my hunger well, moving smoothly from one "addiction" to another, spreading my neediness around, coping with my losses and insecurities by medicating myself with another soporific. This may be as simple and obvious as watching mindless TV (seriously, there is *some* that isn't) or as complex as writing another book.

Yes, Paul's words speak across every demographic ranking. The answer he supplies to his anguished question is this: "Thanks be to God—through Jesus Christ our Lord!" (Rom. 7:25).

What a trite conclusion. At least, it would be if it wasn't so manifestly true.

Repeated drug use depletes the dopamine level in the brain.[1] Dopamine is what allows us to feel pleasure, so the addict is actually killing his or her capacity to enjoy what he or she so strongly craves. Most crack addicts will tell you that the best toke they ever had was the very first one. Part of the reason they keep using is the irrational hope that they'll somehow get back to that magical peak. The more they chase that high, the more remote it becomes.

"It doesn't even do anything for me anymore," one friend told me, his face carved by desolation as if he'd been abandoned by a lover. He was mystified as to why he kept returning to something that was consuming him, chewing him up, body and soul, while giving nothing back.

Strange. The things I so avidly seek have the same effect: I need more and more of them, and they are less and less effective. I know by long and repeated experience that the sources of mental, emotional, and physical pleasure I chase after generally offer only a fleeting "high" at best. If I seek them as a source of joy in and of themselves, they actually deplete my capacity to experience joy. This is true even if they are legitimate pursuits—for example, job recognition or material comforts aren't wrong or bad unless they are sought for their own sake and made the fundamental means of fulfilling us.

On the other hand, when Jesus is the route I travel toward fulfillment, I find exactly the opposite. (Remember? He called himself "the Way" [John 14:6]: the path, the road, the route you travel to get There.) When I seek him, root my values and desires in him, when I found my relationships and sense of self on him, my capacity for joy increases. The more I "have" Jesus, the deeper my enjoyment of him. He increases my desire for those things that are good, adds value to that which is benign, and diminishes the strength of the negative (the evil) that threatens to throttle me. My dependence on material values and experiences as the means by which I define or please myself decreases.

If Jesus is the Way, God must be "There"—the Destination. Home. "In my Father's house are many rooms.… I am going there to prepare a place for you" (John 14:2).

My heart just breaks when I think that Benny's early experiences of "home" were so impoverished that he chose, very deliberately and by radical action, a federal penitentiary as the best available place to fulfill those universal longings for health, wholeness, dignity, security, fellowship, and meaning. It breaks for the robbery done to his imagination, the violence done to his spirit, the perverseness of the relationships that shaped him. It breaks, too, because we at Sanctuary could not be the home he so desperately needed.

Another friend of mine experiences shorter but more frequent "vacations" at government expense. When he gets out of jail, Sanctuary is usually the first place he heads for. He'll poke his head through a doorway and announce, with a grin that's half little boy and half wicked, "I'm home!"

It's charming and touching because, as he and others have often said to me, Sanctuary is the closest thing to home that he knows and we are more like family to him than his own blood relations. But the truth, for him and for me, is that the places we call home—places where we feel welcomed and where we feel we belong: a really good church or work community; the houses, apartments, or stairwells we live in; the country, the city where we were born or which we adopted—these places are really more like stopping points along the way. They are the echoes of a dimly heard melody that sets our spirits briefly soaring before it is swallowed up in the cacophony of our lives. They are like a Rembrandt painting cheaply reproduced and cut up into odd-shaped bits. We collect and sort the bits, slowly piecing them together, gradually getting a kind of a flat, discolored version of the whole richer, grander, deeper, broader picture we know in our gut is out there somewhere, but which we have yet to see.

I know so much less now than I did twenty-five years ago. Knowing was more important to me then—the certainty of fact, the careful boundaries of doctrine. These days, my life is more characterized by longing. The kind of knowing I value now is the slow, subtle knowingness of intimacy. This longing seems to point me more truly and consistently "There" than the confidence of being right ever did.

I used to think that God was sending me to the streets to introduce people to him. Now I think he was prying me away from my certainties so I could meet him in a new and deeper way. I used to think that, out of the richness of my spiritual and social condition, I could bless the poor. I had read the Bible many times through, studied it for years, and somehow never realized—not truly—that it is the poor who are blessed in God's kingdom. That I was the one who needed his blessing.

As a good evangelical Christian who believed that the gospel was all about my personal salvation, I missed the import of Jesus announcing that he had been anointed to "preach good news to the poor" (Luke 4:18). More careful students than I tell me that there are more than 2,000 references in more than four hundred different passages of Scripture that speak of God's passion for the poor. My own studies reveal to me that, in the Hebrew alone, biblical writers use more than forty different words to describe conditions of poverty. These roughly sort into four primary categories, indicating destitution or dispossession, oppression, affliction (suffering, depression, helplessness), and sickness (diminished strength, disease). Beyond that, there are terms that describe the people and conditions that are likely to indicate poverty or exclusion: the widow, orphan, foreigner, hungry, weak, naked, homeless, etc.

I read somewhere once that the Inuit peoples of the Canadian Territories and Alaska (often called "Eskimo") have a similar number of words to label different kinds of snow. If you knew absolutely nothing else about the Inuit, that one fact would tell you that they live in a very cold climate and that snow is profoundly important to them. God's lexical extravagance regarding issues of poverty sends me the same message: Poor people have a critical place at the very heart of God's relationship with humanity.

I'm thrilled—really, although I often take it for granted, "thrilled" is exactly the right word—that the death and resurrection of Jesus guarantees that I am saved, forgiven for all the nonsense I get up to, set free from the dominating power of sin in my life, welcomed into God's family, and promised a true and eternal home. This is one of the few things I still think I "know." This is at the heart of my personal relationship with God.

There are many more biblical passages dealing with poverty than with personal salvation, however, and this reminds me that my relationship with my world—my social being—needs to be rooted in the gospel Jesus said he had come to proclaim, a gospel that is about freedom for prisoners, sight for the blind, relief for the oppressed. That's what the Bible calls "justice." "Justice" is often mistranslated as "righteousness." And in our contemporary society, what we usually mean by "justice" is "vengeance." Biblical justice is a matter of neither moral piety nor retribution, but of treating people rightly in the first place and making sure that those whose opportunities to live well have been restricted or removed are restored to spiritual, physical, economic, and political health and freedom.

I grew up in a home where I was welcomed and loved, provided with everything I needed (including instruction in the miracle of God's grace through Jesus and my own deep need of it), not to mention a healthy measure of what I merely wanted. Like most children and a great many adults, I assumed that my circumstances were normal— that the many goods and experiences I enjoyed were to be expected. If I thought of them at all, I suppose I thought that the life conditions of the six billion or so people in this world who have far, far less than me were abnormal. Furthermore, I really believed that I was entitled to everything I had and often even that I had earned it. Although I can remember my father quoting Psalms as he gave thanks for meals—"The lines are fallen unto me in pleasant places; yea, I have a goodly heritage" (Ps. 16:6 KJV)—I had only the merest sense of just how incredibly advantaged I was.

I could see that there were a lot of people over "there" somewhere who were caught in unfortunate circumstances, circumstances they had done nothing to deserve and about which they could do very little. But like most wealthy first worlders, I really thought that the poor people in my own patch must be lazy, rebellious, wrongheaded, willfully ignorant, or more sinful than most. In short, I thought they must be the architects of their own misfortune.

Of course, I also never thought of myself as rich. Do you know anybody who does? Most of the wealthiest people I know would describe themselves as "comfortable," or, if pressed, "well off." When asked by a reporter just how much one needed these days to be rich, the fabulously wealthy Lord Beaverbrook responded, "Just a little more."

When I began in "full-time ministry" in 1992, I felt pretty heroic about the fact that my family of six was risking living on donations, embracing about a 40 percent reduction in annual income. If I thought of myself as "almost getting by" up to that point, now I felt we were about to descend into a kind of noble poverty.

But then I began to spend every day walking the streets, hanging out with people who wore their entire wardrobe, slept in cardboard boxes, and dropped hints of childhood experiences in "normal" middle-class suburban homes that had sent them spinning into cycles of destruction. Their current destitution was the sum of a grisly equation in which affliction (say, an abusive parent) was added to oppression (like the systematic destruction of aboriginal culture and family structures by government and church) and sickness (perhaps mental illness or a raging addiction), leading to material destitution.

A while ago, somebody sent me the link to an interesting Web site. I typed my yearly income into the little box provided, pressed enter, and discovered that I was even wealthier than I had dreamed. Apparently, I rank in the top 1.5 percent of people in the world in terms of personal wealth. I had been feeling quite self-righteous about the fact that I was still making less than I had fifteen years earlier as a carpenter. Suddenly, I discovered that I rank in the world's elite. I had never been in the top 1 percent of anything before! I have to admit, it felt pretty good. I was tempted to see about having an opera house or a boulevard named after me.

Mind you, the Web site also told me that some fifty-seven million other people were richer than me. I'm still a little bitter about that, but I'm getting over it.

The point is this: If you live in a first world nation, you're probably richer than 98 or 99 percent of the world's inhabitants. If you bought this book yourself, or borrowed it from a peer who did (Shame! Buy your own copy, you cheapskate! My publisher and I need just a little more …), you're likely a penthouse dweller on the world's economic scale. If you hold title to a house or an automobile, even if you have years and years of payments ahead of you, you're definitely the cream of the crop.

The terms "rich" and "poor" in the subtitle and throughout this book are a convenient, admittedly oversimplistic, black-and-white, and possibly even pejorative shorthand, dividing the world's population neatly into one tiny little group and one huge one. I'll claim some justification by pointing out that Jesus often used extreme images to make a point too: "If your eye causes you to sin, pluck it out" (Mark 9:47). "If anyone comes to me and does not hate his father and mother, his wife and children, his brothers and sisters—yes, even his own life— he cannot be my disciple" (Luke 14:26).

The reality, of course, is that the rich are usually, because of their riches, barely conscious of their deep poverty and the consequent invitation to embrace their true identity in relationship with their Maker that can be found only in those depths. And the poor (at least in a first world culture) generally have little sense of their blessedness, the amazing gifts they have to share with people who appear to them to already have it all.

As I've said, I used to think the poor were themselves the primary reason for their own poverty. Then I began to understand that they were usually victims of oppressive relationships, situations, and systems that were beyond their control. *So*, I thought, *the rich need to get in there and save the poor!* I began to feel that the rich (except for me and a few friends, of course) were all heartless and needed saving more than my poor friends. For a while, I was convinced that the rich actually needed the poor more than the poor needed them. (Still a tempting but essentially selfish position.)

And now I've come to this simple conclusion: We need each other.

In fact, I believe that God urges the rich and powerful to care for the poor and vulnerable throughout Scripture because we each have what the other needs. He is so adamant and voluble about it that I must conclude that we can hardly expect to get "There" unless we travel the Way together.

We are guiding each other on the way home.

CHAPTER 5

ON THE WAY

Were not our hearts burning within us while he talked
with us on the road and opened the Scriptures to us?
—Luke 24:32

There are two Rembrandt paintings hanging in the Louvre that depict the moment at which two disciples, having walked some eighteen or nineteen miles[1] from Jerusalem to Emmaus in the company of a stranger—a stranger with a surprising, unorthodox, thrilling understanding of the Old Testament prophets—realize that he is Jesus himself.

I've been to the Louvre only once and can hardly wait to go back. The Rembrandt gallery was what I was most looking forward to, and I have to confess that I didn't linger very long in the preceding large hall given to a series of massive paintings by Rubens: acres of pale voluptuous flesh, billows of rich cloth, cherubs, and elaborate wigs; improbably mythical scenarios depicting the birth and early life of the Sun King; and prominently featuring, since she commissioned the paintings, his mother, Marie Therese, and her breasts.

The Rembrandt room seemed at first a small, poor thing in comparison. It was the size of a suburban living room, square, a doorway at each end. The *Mona Lisa*, alone, had three times the space devoted to it. Hung about the walls were perhaps a dozen smallish, mostly dark paintings. None of them were a tenth the size of the Rubens and not nearly as dashing, colorful, or ebullient. Still, I sat there for an hour looking at Rembrandt's muddy little paintings and could not keep from weeping.

There were two "pairs" of paintings I remember and loved best— pairs in the sense that in each case the subject was the same, but the treatment of it was separated by about thirty years of life experience on the part of the artist. One set was self-portraits, the other the paintings of the electric moment when Jesus was revealed in the breaking of bread.

The first self-portrait features a young, bold, proud Rembrandt dressed in brocaded velvet robes, a rich burgher's hat on his head, and a heavy gold chain around his neck. The artist with the twirling mustache stares back at the viewer with a self-satisfied arrogance that borders on aggression. It's a brilliant painting, fairly crackling with a sense of the young painter's genius. It's thought that he was in his early thirties when he painted it, and his sense of the promise his life holds, the expectation that it will be fulfilled, probably very soon, is palpable.

On the other side of the room was perhaps his last self-portrait, thought to have been executed within a year or eighteen months of his death. He looks like a beaten man or one of my elderly friends from the street: a rag tied around his balding head, three days' growth of patchy beard, a dark, paint-spattered smock that blends into the indeterminate darkness wrapping around his figure. One shadowy hand holds a paintbrush, the other a barely visible palette and a few more brushes. The edge of an easel borders the right-hand side of the painting. Except for his face, the image is mostly hints and general-izations, as if to say, "The details no longer matter."

And what a face! His head alone reflects light—in fact, in that classic trick of late Rembrandt, it seems that his head is the source of light. But half his face remains in shadow; no trace here of arrogance, self-satisfaction, or even expectation. There is no beauty here that we should desire him; not, at least, in any conventional sense.

It is, however, the revelation of a man who, through suffering and poverty, through the failure of his dreams, has come to know who he really is and who, in the knowing, has made peace with himself and God. There are pain and quiet joy in his dark eyes (looking past the viewer) and in the set of his mouth, a gentleness and wisdom utterly absent from the earlier painting.

Although I don't know the salient facts (I'm no art historian[2]), it's hard to imagine that this work found a buyer in his lifetime or even that he painted it with the hope of selling it. There is no flash or performance here; it's like those rare moments when a musician of extravagant talent plinks out a few notes on the piano, sings quietly in the middle of her range, unconscious of the audience, and you know the music is coming from the deepest well of her soul. This is art at its very peak, the summation of a life journey, perhaps the deepest wisdom a human being may have and impart. "Here I am," this Rembrandt seems to whisper. "Take it or leave it—it doesn't really matter. I finally have found myself, and none of the trappings signify."

There's a similar gap between the early and late paintings of the Emmaus road disciples. The 1648 *Supper at Emmaus* is a lovely paint-ing full of light. A typical bearded Christ sits at a table beside a window in a tall, colonnaded room. Although the sun beams onto him and the table from the viewer's left, he is also clearly haloed; his eyes are raised piously toward heaven, and his head has that sideways tilt common to early iconography. One disciple sits on each side of him, and a servant is in the act of bending to place a plate of food on the table. It's the dramatic moment of the revelation of the identity of the mystery guest: As Jesus breaks the bread, the disciple on his right is raising a hand to his mouth in astonishment; the one on his left is physically taken aback.

It's an explicitly religious scene. And, although the composition of the figures is similar, the tone of the painting couldn't be more different than that of *The Pilgrims at Emmaus*. The date of this painting is uncertain, but it was definitely much later than *The Supper at Emmaus* and, again, probably painted within the last few years of Rembrandt's life. Even the change in titles seems to indicate a different perspective, as if the painter had come to understand that the event itself was less significant than the journey.

There's a change in physical perspective too: The viewer witnesses the scene in the earlier painting from above, a position removed and omniscient. Lofty. The viewer of *Pilgrims* is nearer, perhaps just across the room, and at the level of or even slightly below the table at which Jesus and the disciples sit. There is no server, but an enigmatic figure—Rembrandt himself?—watches the proceedings from deep shadow at the right side and behind the others. There are no arches or columns, no airy space above the figures, which are themselves poorer, less theatrical, a little tatty. The sunshine entering through a mullioned window at the left diffuses hardly at all: The back of one disciple and the right shoulder of Christ are brightly lit, but all else is dim. Even the face and hands of Jesus are in shadow. There is no iconic posture here: His head is slightly bowed, his hands are at rest, the bread is obscure. The disciples seem to be recognizing him slowly, rather than in a flash of revelation, like a faded memory gradually acquiring details from the brain's most distant vaults—"Oh yeah, hmm, I think I … wait a second, isn't that …?"

There's nothing overtly religious about this scene. But for the title, it could be any three people chatting casually over a meal. And there is an intimacy, a depth, an organic nature to this picture that invites you in, encourages you to wonder, offers you rest in a way that the earlier painting does not.

Rembrandt painted this scene at least three times. I'm convinced he imagined, in great detail and with increasing insight through the difficult later years of his own life, the long, confusing, heartbroken outward trudge of the two pilgrims. The appearance of their mysterious companion; his astonishing, strangely healing, and perhaps slightly impatient teaching about the true nature and mission of the Messiah. The piercing moment when he broke the bread and their grave-bound faith was resurrected. Their immediate, excited return journey, all weariness having disappeared, to the city from which they had fled. Their wide-eyed description to "the [remaining] Eleven," themselves still stunned by the shock of Jesus' execution, of how he had appeared to them—two unimportant, halfhearted disciples who had been ready to give up the whole thing! And, finally, the appearance again of the One they longed for, this time to all of them (save Thomas) at once.

I believe that the young, supremely confident painter, who just knew he had almost arrived, learned, through the course of many painful years, that movement is the thing. He learned that we grow only by letting go of those things that protect us, or confirm our importance, or justify to ourselves our attitudes and actions, and moving forward into the shadows, where faith is the substance of things hoped for and the evidence of things unseen. The eyes that look calmly past the viewer in Rembrandt's last self-portrait are contemplating the next steps—who knows how many little, stumbling steps?—and beyond them, the last great leap from Here to There. The painter of *The Pilgrims at Emmaus* understands now that a humbler perspective is a deeper one, that the shadows of uncertainty are the breeding ground of true faith, and that a pilgrim never, in this life, "arrives."

Although in my pride or in my destitution I may convince myself otherwise, I do not journey alone. There are companions on the road, and Christ himself will show up to guide me, though I may not recognize him at first. I hurry. I drag behind. I stagger or, for a time, run lightly. My heart burns within me, but I do not know what it means. He appears—a momentary glimpse—and is gone. I move on, musing over this brief, mysterious unveiling of the Divine, asking myself as I go what it means. To me? To my world? In time I may ask myself, "Did it really happen? Was it just a figment of my imagination?" For me, one "unveiling" can never be enough.

But all the time I am moving. From isolation to intimacy. From productivity to fruitfulness. From suffering to glory.

FROM ISOLATION TO INTIMACY

And the Lord God said, "It is not good for the man to be alone."
—Genesis 2:18

DAVE

The pale late October sun had been dodging clouds all day, but now it gave up and slipped behind the tall office buildings that pillared the intersection of Yonge and St. Clair.

It must be just after five, he thought—funny how the streets were so suddenly full of cars, and scuttling pedestrians seemed to sprout instantaneously from the sidewalk. The press of vehicles was irrelevant though, unless he should accidentally step backward off the curb into the traffic. The people hustling from their offices and stores were his mark. He stood with his heels planted on the outer rim of that curb, as far out as possible so that the cops had no excuse to ticket him for obstructing the sidewalk—not that it would keep them from doing it anyway, although, to be fair, they weren't nearly as aggressive here as they had been downtown. Some were even friendly, checking on him in his squat from time to time to make sure he was still breathing and not hassling him even if they found him, as they had once or twice, with a crack pipe in his hand. He flipped up his cardboard sign and gave the coins in the bottom of his coffee cup a little rattle.

Best to be out here on the edge for visibility too, he thought. Too easy for people to miss you if you were standing with your back up against a busy store window. And the sign helped some, though not the way it once did:

Canadian Vietnam vet
spare some change for food and shelter

Most people could avoid his eyes easily, staring intently over his shoulder as if searching for a sail on the horizon. But some couldn't keep from reading the message scrawled in black Magic Marker on the square he had torn carefully from a box nicked from the stack behind Sobey's. The sign was months old now, and looked it. The rim of it had grown thin and acquired a low luster where he held it most often; the words had faded some. An old sign was more effective than a new one, in his opinion. It let people know he'd been around awhile, wasn't just some backwoods boy who had got lost in the big city. The longer he had a sign, the more he liked it; it began to feel like a friend of sorts, and he was always disconcerted and cranky for a few days when he had to make a new one.

There was a period—oh, ten or fifteen years ago—when being a Vietnam vet had been a good thing. People had finally gotten over blaming the grunts for government stupidity, and movies like *Coming Home,*

The Deer Hunter, Platoon, and his own favorite, *Apocalypse Now*, had made the poor slobs who had slogged through the jungle and the rice paddies into, well, if not exactly heroes, then at least legitimate tragic figures. Story of his life, *Apocalypse Now* was. He'd seen it a dozen times, paying once and sitting through four or five showings in a row. Dropping a little acid for old time's sake. Even back then, couples would edge along the row of folded-up seats toward where he sat at dead center of the theater, get a close look at him, and suddenly decide aisle seats were a better choice.

Forces vets or guys currently serving would still read the sign and dig deep, but even they didn't ask questions about his service anymore. And the average citizen, including the ones who actually read the sign, didn't seem to register it at all. Ancient history now, Vietnam. Probably mostly a waste of time, that sign, but it did save him from having to call out, "Spare some change?" over and over.

He had a few regulars, people who would stuff a five or even, big thrill, a twenty in his cup once a week, but none of them were coming by today. Quarters, loonies, and toonies.[1] Sometimes the dregs of a pocket or purse: pennies, nickels, and dimes—useless these days for actually purchasing anything and an annoyance to carry around. They made a difference to him, though, and local convenience store owners were glad to have them for making change. They'd happily give him paper money for what he collected in the course of a day (his dealer would refuse to take twenty dollars in coins), and one Korean woman had been doing it so long she would simply ask, "How much you got?" and hand over the bills without bothering to count the coins.

People streamed by, their faces set and remote. Some who saw him from ten or fifteen feet away made subtle shifts in direction so they could pass him by on the inner lane of the sidewalk, with a buffer of other pedestrians between them. Most who dropped money into his cup did so without a word or making eye contact. A few smiled and said hello or an apologetic "It's all I have." Regardless, he thanked each one politely, addressing them as sir or ma'am.

There were fewer jerks here, uptown, than there had been in Yorkville or farther down Yonge Street—just normal working people mostly, not young party animals or rich snobs, so it was easier to be polite. He had slugged a movie star outside Remy's one time four or five years ago. The snotty, coked-up pretty boy had thrown a handful of pennies at him and told him where to go. When the little goof had dragged himself up off the pavement, bleeding a bit and threatening mayhem, the club bouncer moved forward and informed the actor he'd best step into the waiting limo and make himself scarce. Astonishment. Fury. Impotent, babbling indignation. It was a good memory.

Fewer street animals, too. He missed the fraternity of being farther south, working simple street cons, pooling resources, and getting high together with other guys (and the occasional woman); but, much as he hated to admit it, he couldn't stand the pace anymore. He no longer had the patience to deal with their crazy stunts, nor the physical strength to deal with the certainty that one of the other crackhead clowns, or a Listerine-fueled Indian, or even one of his own mates gone all tizic (a response to sustained crack use that fries the user's synapses and nerves so that they fire random, spastic messages even when he or she isn't high) would sooner or later go off on him. One might even coldcock him with a two-by-four for the change in his cup or the twenty-piece in his pocket. If those boys got a sniff of the fact that you didn't have the energy to hunt them down and exact a terrible retribution, you were a marked man. He'd seen guys go from confident protectors of their own turf to concussion-addled punching bags in a matter of months. It was never long, then, until they would be found curled up and stone-cold dead in a doorway or stairwell.

No, it was better to be alone.

He stood there, shifting from foot to foot as unobtrusively as possible. His knees were killing him, and his left foot (a couple of toes lost to frostbite the winter before last), but he didn't want to look like some antic, dancing fool. Might attract attention that way, but it would scare people off.

The pedestrian traffic was dwindling now anyway. It was getting dark, and he could feel the approach of winter in the wind that came humming up the hill. He poured the change out of the cup into his palm, bounced it once or twice, counting it automatically and mentally adding it to what he had already transferred to his pocket. It was enough. A short, square-shouldered figure with shaggy hair and a fine beard, he turned and limped across the intersection.

He bought a burger and a drink at the McDonald's in the subway entrance and carried it down the street toward his squat. He already had a twenty-piece carefully folded into a square of paper and tucked away. Surprising how, these days, just having a piece in reserve was often enough. He probably wouldn't even smoke it before going to sleep—might just keep it in case he needed it in the night or to get him going in the morning.

Pausing on the sidewalk, he looked casually around to see if anyone was watching before taking a few quick steps and ducking under an angled concrete abutment attached to an apartment building. There were a piece of foam, a couple of sleeping bags, and a plastic bag with a few items of clothing tucked behind the sheet of plywood he had found by the apartment Dumpster. The plywood provided privacy and a windscreen; and best of all, it looked like it actually belonged there. He lit the candle melted onto a ledge in the concrete, unfolded his bedding, and sat down to eat.

The trees in the ravine beside the apartment building had lost most of their leaves. He liked seeing them first thing when he woke up in the morning. They reminded him of his aunt's cottage up in the Muskokas, the beautiful lake and silent pines where he had spent his summers as a kid, during his parents' troubles. He imagined for the umpteenth time that he would call her in the spring, hitchhike up there, and borrow the canoe and a fishing rod. Spend the summer in the bush. It had been years since they had talked—he was almost sixty himself—hard to believe. How old would that make Aunt Alma? Last winter had been the first that he'd wondered if he would make it to spring.

He finished his Coke, wadded the burger wrapper and bag into the cup, and pitched it into the darkness past his feet. A gust of wind rattled the plywood but left him untouched. He took off his shoes and jacket, climbed halfway into his sleeping bag, and blew out the candle.

Lying back, he imagined the apartment building soaring twenty stories above him. He imagined the families, couples old and young, single men and women, throwing aside their coats and checking their voice mail, making supper, flipping on the TV, or contemplating what movie to see or pub to hang out in later in the evening. He knew none of them, but the weight of their lives pressed down on him, pushing him deeper into the darkness.

MARK

Standing in front of the open dishwasher, he drained his orange juice and placed the glass on the upper rack, then gave Judith a peck on the back of the neck. She dropped one side of the newspaper to run a hand down his departing arm. Peering over her reading glasses—how did she manage to look elegant wearing an old dressing gown, bed-head, and reading glasses?—she bid him good-bye and the earliest possible return, the usual mantra delivered in her usual faintly growly morning voice.

Moments later Mark was pulling out of the driveway. Before he hit the first stop sign, he had enabled Bluetooth and was asking his car to retrieve all phone and e-mail messages from his BlackBerry. He got off the highway as soon as he could and onto Lakeshore Drive. It was slower, but closer to the lake (a fabulous cobalt blue on this beautiful spring morning), and he justified the longer commute by his communion with the BlackBerry. It was a profitable, pleasant, and almost leisurely drive into the city.

For years, he had routinely been the first one to arrive at work, convinced of the value of setting a stainless steel example for his employees and, he could admit to his friends now, out of a sheer, panicky, and usually unreasonable conviction that the company could fail at any moment. Now, although he still arrived no later than 9:30 and almost always stayed until at least 6:00, he considered his "late" arrival a subtle daily statement to his employees and those of his peers who were at their desks by 7:00 a.m. (Mark would smile and lift his chin when they accused him with jocular voices and jealous eyes of getting soft and lazy) that the company was strong, secure, solvent, unfazed by the competition. The company address—an entire floor of BCE Place, at Bay and Wellington in the very heart of the Canadian financial galaxy—his cars, his house, his "cottage" in the Muskokas (worth millions), his trips, and his quietly expensive suits all delivered the same message.

Parking the Lexus in his reserved spot ("CEO, Smyth-Barron"), he unplugged the BlackBerry, put on his suit jacket, and retrieved his briefcase from the passenger seat. A brief moment of wordless prayer waiting for the elevator that delivered him from P2 to the main lobby. With his head high and a forthright, cheerful expression on his face, he crossed the marbled surface of the lobby to the elevator dedicated to those floors numbering twenty to thirty.

He entered the elevator—*empty, thank you, God*—and as the mahogany-paneled doors closed before him, the old panic began to gnaw at his gut. The car rose swiftly, soundlessly, and the LCD screen above the buttons burbled the current NASDAQ, Dow, and TSX information at him. The pressure increased as if the elevator was pushing him upward against an intractable downward force.

A remote woman's voice announced his imminent arrival at his company's floor—arrival at the invariable, hellish, absolutely worst moment of every working day these past twenty years. The most worrisome of the e-mail and phone messages that had piled up over the weekend, the nasty lawsuit that was brewing, unfavorable financial forecasts, tension between a bright young staff person and a manager who was proving incompetent, the knowledge that his closest competitor had just hired a headhunter to source precisely the kind of executive represented by the employee he most depended upon and with an offer he probably couldn't match. These and a host of other anxieties assailed him like an army of tiny demons shrieking in his ear. Beneath them the dull, thudding voice that had pursued him since he dared to open up shop and declare himself the boss: "The company is going to fail. *You* are going to fail. If you let *anyone* know, they will abandon you, and it will fail immediately ..."

Even after all these years, Judith knew nothing of this moment, this almost daily moment, particularly sharp on Mondays. He had tried to tell her once, but it had frightened her—she didn't understand that he was talking about his irrational fears, not the actual situation, and thought he meant the company was really failing. He covered up immediately, apologized for upsetting her with a bad joke, and never mentioned it again.

His employees didn't know about it either. At the merest whiff of this kind of panic they would begin to drift away. Even Jacques, Mark's right-hand man, who knew firsthand the factual, objective truth of the company's solidity, who could be counted on to resist the temptations offered by the headhunter, and at least discuss them with him if they grew too great—even Jacques would jump without hesitation if he sensed this awful, roiling, irrational fear in his boss.

The elevator pinged; the doors slid open. Mark squared his shoulders and stepped out, perfect in his isolation: calm, authoritative, impenetrable.

CHAPTER 6

INTIMACY AND ISOLATION

Terrified of being alone, yet afraid of intimacy, we experience widespread
feelings of emptiness, of disconnection, of the unreality of self.
—*Sherry Turkle,* The Second Self

Except a corn of wheat fall into the ground
and die, it abideth alone.
—*Jesus, John 12:24 KJV*

Desire for intimacy must be one of the greatest of human urges. It keeps us seeking romance even when we've been disappointed, believing in the concept of marriage when so many fail, keeps us open to new friendships when we know every friend will let us down sooner or later, and impels us to have kids when we remember how we broke our own parents' hearts. The mere illusion of it can sometimes keep us in abusive relationships until health, wealth, and even life itself are gone. The absence of the desire or capacity for intimacy seems so wrong to us that we describe people so afflicted as being subject to personality disorders. We were made for intimacy, with both our Creator and our fellow creatures, and it's the most fulfilling of human experiences.

The story of humanity as told in the Bible is the story of God's successive attempts to heal the breaches we continually cause and restore us to intimate relationship with himself. Jesus declares in John's gospel his own heart's great desire for humanity: "that all of them may be one, Father, just as you are in me and I am in you.... Father, I want those you have given me to be with me where I am" (John 17:21, 24).

This intimacy has been at the heart of the reflections of the church's great mystics and devotional writers throughout history (Julian of Norwich, Teresa of Ávila, Thomas à Kempis, John of the Cross, and more recently Henri Nouwen, Jean Vanier, and John Eldredge among others). When they speak of knowing God, they do not mean assembling as many facts about him as possible, but rather knowing him as a lover knows her mate. In fact, there's a lovely Old Testament convention, lost in more modern versions but quite accurately rendered in the King James Version, of describing sex in exactly those terms: "Adam *knew* Eve his wife; and she conceived" (Gen. 4:1 KJV). Clearly, deep intimacy between two individuals is a potent and fruitful venture!

Ironically, true intimacy is probably also one of our greatest fears. Most of us spend a tremendous amount of time, energy, and money on creating an image of ourselves to sell to the world around us—an image based on what we would like to believe about ourselves, if we didn't know better. An image more acceptable, we hope, than the unlovely self we are sure would be rejected if it was discovered. Fearing to be truly known, we hoist that image and carry it before us like a shield, protecting the vulnerable, tender inner core where we truly dwell. The more we succumb to this fear, the deeper we descend into isolation and the more convinced we become that we must hide the "awful truth" about our deepest selves.

To compound the matter, we discover quickly that even the people closest to us experience the same events differently. I am the youngest of three brothers. Although we come from the same gene pool, grew up in the same home, and shared many experiences as kids, each of us felt and processed the recent death of our father in very different ways, as we did his actual fathering. My four children, to whom I am so intimately connected in every imaginable way, and Karen, with whom I shared a quarter of a century of married life, and I each experienced the dissolution of that marriage in a way that left us, to differing degrees, feeling isolated and lonely. Even the simple experience of watching a movie together, or reading the same book, often reveals how widely we differ in our perceptions. Shared experience, then, is not always enough to create intimacy.

We are born of the most intimate physical act, but our souls walk alone. Apart from execution, isolation is one of the most severe forms of punishment there is and a most effective form of torture. (Think of Steve McQueen in the isolation cell on Devil's Island in the movie *Papillon*.) We spend much of our lives longing and striving to escape the dank cell of emotional isolation so that we can move freely in the broad, colorful world of meaningful human relationship.

People who are poor are often painfully aware of their exclusion from much of what we value in the Western world. My friends who, like Dave, panhandle to survive daily experience "normal" people walking past, looking past, or looking through them as if they didn't exist at all. Even the money they receive sometimes comes at the cost of a pitying or condescending look, harsh language, and the not-so-helpful suggestion, "Get a job!" They're used to being chased from place to place, and almost always deeper into obscurity, by the police and city bylaws—often under pressure from business improvement or home owners' associations that want to "clean up" their patch of the city.

To some rich people who have never truly met them, my poor friends are disfiguring cancers on the face of the city, unsightly blemishes to be removed as expeditiously as possible, with little concern about where or to what they are to be removed—and little care about what awful personal storms have washed them up on that bit of sidewalk in the first place. Out of sight, out of mind. (I speak in broad generalities; there are many individual business owners who are deeply concerned about people who are poor and are committing significant amounts of energy and resource to find solutions.) In Toronto, this means breaking up any large gathering of homeless people and chasing them into the ravines, alleys, and shadows beneath the bridges and expressway off-ramps. In many other North American cities, it means herding people into ghettos that can be so depressed they look like war zones.

My homeless friends are not the only ones who experience such isolation. People who are rich may be unaware of how contained and narrow their lives have become. Some, like Mark, may discover that success itself has trapped and isolated them. Gated communities, security systems, and houses situated on properties large enough to keep the inhabitants as far as possible from the neighbors are markers of the ghettoization of people who are wealthy and powerful even by Western standards. The glitterati, whose every move and foible (infidelity! cellulite!) are trumpeted by print and television tabloids, are held hostage and sometimes destroyed by the fame they have so avidly sought.

Even those of us who are rich only in the average middle-class Western world manner can find ourselves isolated. Even in the church. Maybe especially in the church.

Some years ago, in the course of a speaking engagement at a large church in north Toronto, I told the audience about my friendship with Neil, a gay man who had died of AIDS.[1] It was, at the time, pretty exotic fare for a middle-class, suburban, conservative evangelical congregation. It became even more so when I described to them how I had come to see that Jesus was making himself present to me through Neil, just a few days before his death, and in a way that was, for Neil, messy, excruciating, and humiliating. Although the audience was attentive and even affirming, I felt keenly how little I had been able to communicate of Neil's beauty and power in that moment and how very separate I seemed from those listeners to whom homosexuality was a cipher in a complex doctrinal equation and AIDS a nightmare visited only upon people far away and faceless.

That sense of my own isolation paled shortly after Dorothy put her hand on my arm, out in the lobby, and looked up at me with eyes glistening with contained emotion. I had known Dorothy when I was a teenager, but I hadn't seen her in years. She thanked me for speaking about Neil in a positive, dignifying way, and then she dropped her bomb.

"My Joe," she said, and stopped, glancing quickly around to make sure no one else was within earshot. "My Joe is dying of AIDS."

I remembered arguing passionately with Joe, who had claimed David Bowie (in his Ziggy Stardust days; that's how long ago it was) to be the brightest and boldest star in the musical firmament. I had scorned Bowie's antics and costumes as mere posturing and lifted high the name of Bob Dylan as the one true iconic genius of the age.

I expressed my genuine dismay to Dorothy and my sympathy for her. I asked the appropriate questions regarding Joe's current health, treatment, state of mind and soul, prognosis, and so on. She seemed both reluctant and relieved to talk about it, standing quite close to me and speaking almost in a whisper. I wondered how she and her daughters were dealing with it. Tears lapped against her lower lashes, threatening her mascara, but she blinked them away as she spoke. I can imagine nothing worse than watching one of my four children die. I could almost hear her heart breaking.

What about other supports for her? I asked. Was the church holding her through this brutal ordeal?

Her eyes widened. She grimaced faintly.

"Oh no," she murmured. "Nobody here knows. I couldn't tell them. They'd never understand …"

Fifteen hundred followers of the One who embraced and healed all manner of "unclean" people—lepers, blind or crippled beggars, Samaritans, demon-possessed maniacs, Gentile "dogs," women with icky (and ceremonially "defiling") chronic female conditions, even corpses that were already stinky and rotten—and there was nobody she could tell that her son, her only and beloved son, was dying?

I've had this scenario play out often enough in the years since—a parent, usually a mother, sidling up to me to tell me that her son is dying of AIDS, her teenage daughter is hooked on crystal meth and prostituting herself to men old enough to be her father, her eldest is in Kingston doing a seven-year bit for armed robbery *and she can't tell anyone*—to think that Dorothy was likely wrong. In fact, it's entirely likely, given the time period (the mid-'90s, when the North American AIDS epidemic was at its peak) and her church's proximity to one of the largest gay and lesbian communities in the world, that there were a substantial number of other mothers in that very congregation sorrowing over similar issues with their children and similarly convinced they could tell no one. And yet, it's probably also true—don't you think?—that for every one who would have understood Dorothy's pain and wrapped their arms around her, there would be four or five who would carefully avoid her, speaking to each other in shocked whispers of what they had just heard about poor Dorothy's wayward son, Joe.

How much of Dorothy's isolation was due to her own fears, and how much was truly about the character of that particular congregation I don't know. But it's very clear that her anguish was compounded by the fact that she felt so very alone in the middle of it—alone in the middle of her own life situation and doubly alone when sitting in the midst of a large group of (apparently) clean-as-a-whistle, my-life's-in-perfect-order Christians. The great irony, of course, is that every one of us claims to follow Jesus because he is the remedy for our impoverished, sin-stricken souls. "Irony"—no, that's not the right word. It's devilish.

Nevertheless, both Dorothy and I experienced a moment when we moved out of our respective isolations toward a brief but remarkable intimacy. An impeccable, upper-middle-class matron and a long-haired (at the time), living-on-the-edge (relatively speaking) street outreach worker half her age, only marginally acquainted, connected at a deep and healing level. Suddenly, we were not alone in the crowd. Right there in front of each of us was one who "got it," one with whom we did not have to pretend to be fine, thanks.

The guides who called us out of our fearful caves to meet each other were two men afflicted, rejected. Sick and dying. "The poor." And what connected Dorothy and me was not rehearsing our victories, our various points of health and strength—our "wealth"—but the unveiling of our own secret poverty.

The more I learn to step out of my isolation, opening myself to the possibility of intimacy, the less frightening it seems. And yet, I find, it's rarely easy. The hurdles often seem insurmountable. There are many weights to be laid aside so that I can run this marathon race.

My fierce desire for *independence* is particularly insidious because it is seen as such a virtue in our Western world. I want to believe that I can manage it—whether "it" is a task, my emotional, physical, or spiritual needs, a particular life challenge, my relationships with God or other people, or one of a host of other possibilities—on my own. Our popular culture makes "rugged individualism" heroic: Think of the endless list of movie heroes who take matters into their own hands, often against the prevailing wisdom and the societal protections we have so carefully constructed. But this path, I am discovering, leads only to a deeper isolation, a shrinking appetite for spiritual food, the stunting of my soul. The Way of life—the Way I travel with companions like Dorothy, Dave, Mark, Benny, and Arthur—lies in the direction of *communion*.

I find also that I am addicted to *impregnability*—I want to be bulletproof, unassailable. I surround myself with props to heighten the illusion that nothing can take me down. I hustle eagerly toward the next thing that will finally consolidate my position, confirm my power base, guarantee my future. I stack those things around me and peer with increasing smugness over the walls I am building. But when one of my friends coaxes me beyond the walls of my carefully constructed fortress, I begin to discover that it has become a kind of prison. The Way leads to *vulnerability* and true freedom.

CHAPTER 7

FROM INDEPENDENCE TO COMMUNION

We must all hang together, or assuredly we shall all hang separately.
—Benjamin Franklin, at the signing of the Declaration of Independence

They eat, they drink, and in communion sweet
Quaff immortality and joy.
—John Milton, Paradise Lost

The streets are so jammed with revelers that, even on my bicycle, it requires a careful, slow approach to navigate through the bodies clogging the upper end of Church Street and spilling onto Charles.

Pride Week is the biggest event on Toronto's annual tourist calendar—bigger than the Toronto Grand Prix, International Film Festival, or Jazz Festival by far—and the Gay Pride Parade is the biggest event of that week. Close to a million people have hit the streets under a brilliant June sun, watching the parade, dancing to live music, quaffing prodigious quantities of alcohol on bar patios or in temporary beer gardens set up in parking lots, wearing bizarre, sometimes beautiful, and generally skimpy costumes. The queer community has come a long way in terms of public acceptance; having less to prove, the parade and the partying are not quite the over-the-edge bacchanalia they once were—completely naked people or couples simulating sex acts on the parade floats are rarer now—but it's still a wild, riotous, spectacular celebration.

The parade route circles the Sanctuary building. As I weave through the throngs, the tail of it has passed Charles Street going south on Yonge. A thousand spectators are flooding back across Charles to party central on Church Street, the "Main Street" of the rainbow village. Sometimes our group of worshippers sets up tables to pass out water and lemonade on this last Sunday in June, but nobody had the energy this year. The paved front yard of Sanctuary is empty of vehicles, of course: There's no way you'd ever get a car through this crowd. Some of our people, I'm sure, are out there taking in the spectacle; some who come from outlying areas will just stay home, having been caught in the transportation nightmare in previous years. It'll be an even smaller group than usual.

We'll have visitors though, I know. That in itself isn't unusual, but these three will not fall into the usual categories of friends and relatives, youth groups on missions trips, people who have heard or read about Sanctuary somewhere and want to get a firsthand look at it, or Christians who have burnt out on the church and are wondering desperately if Sanctuary might be a last-ditch fit. (These last are not the most common visitors, but they are the ones who usually stay.) That's apart, of course, from homeless people from the neighborhood who might drift in or others who have been nibbling at the edges of our community for long enough to get up the courage to see if they can stand a little of the church stuff.

Drew, a Toronto-based TV guy and spiritual radio talk-show host, arrives about half an hour early with his two protégés: a man and a woman, both in their early twenties, both healthy and handsome, clean, perky, polite, attentive, intelligent. They look like they'd be right at home on the worship team of one of those Next Gen seeker-focused churches. Ironically, they are self-described nonbelievers, and Drew has hired them to be here as part of an experiment. They will visit and assess five different evangelical churches in the Greater Toronto Area on successive Sundays, blog about their experiences,[1] and review what they perceived on Drew's radio show the Saturday after they finish.[2] Together they will observe how we, a small ragtag band of stumblers, "do church—how you do Jesus."

(Drew's words, not mine. I told him we don't "do" church; we're trying to "be" the church; "doing" Jesus in this neighborhood would have a different and distinctly unsavory connotation.)

Drew himself looks like a recently retired linebacker—six four, wide shoulders, square jaw, and a shaved head. Like most talk-show hosts, he is by personality and profession an iconoclast, an "outsider." He describes his mission as finding those who have "holy hand grenades" up their butts and pulling the pin. Although he has spent his adult life in "full-time ministry" in churches, Christian camps, and youth-focused organizations before radio and TV, he has for several years now been dumping on the church from ever-greater heights. This is, I think, because of his deep love for Jesus—who, inconveniently, loves the church. It's kind of a "love me, love my people" sort of thing. Sometimes he'll trot out the old Augustine quote: "The church is a whore—but she's my mother!"

"*I am frustrated* and actually, *yes ... I am* angry," Drew says. "Very angry, at how Christian leaders have been allowed to consistently get away with selling a North American, narcissistic, insular, materialistic, 'what's in it for me,' squeaky clean, sterile Christianity…. 'I want to tell you about my God, but before I tell you about him, you have to come to my fortress …'"

Although he won't be happy to be described this way, Drew is in many ways like an Old Testament prophet, standing back from God's people and putting an annoying finger on their sore spots. (What's with people who actually *want* to be described as prophets these days? Haven't they read about the kinds of things that happened to those old-timers?) And he's as hard on himself as he is on others, describing himself as "spiritually uncoordinated, phenomenally insecure … my spiritual disciplines are hopeless … the number one thing Jesus has done in my life is he hasn't quit on me."

Drew has made the one-hour commute (much longer on Pride Sunday) from his family home in Orangeville, a quaint town northwest of the city, surrounded by farms, horse breeders, and maple sugar bush. It's a far cry from the press of oiled, painted, and be-feathered bodies he and his pagan acolytes have made their way through to get here.

Standing in the middle of Sanctuary's paved front yard is a burly young man with a wild thicket of hair. He is sketching, stopping every few strokes of the pencil to look up at the front of the building. When Drew sidles around behind him to take a look, he finds the image the man has drawn bears no relationship at all to what he is looking at. We're not in Kansas anymore, Toto.

My friend Ken, on the other hand, lives right in the middle of this craziness, in a tiny one-bedroom apartment where books—carefully sorted and of every imaginable genre—command far more space than furniture. This morning he woke up excited and looking forward to the day: His birthday and the Pride celebrations are aligned.

Birthdays are important to most of us. They remind us that we're unique and, if we are so blessed, that we are surrounded by family and friends who care about us. There will be no family party for Ken. Hardly anybody even knows it's his birthday. He will only mention it to me a week and a half later, and he won't make a big deal of it. Nevertheless, it's perhaps a more important day to him than it is to most people.

When Ken was born, his parents were told that their new little boy might possibly live to five years of age. They looked at his deformities and abandoned him for good. He has never met his mother or his father.

For those first five years, he never left the hospital. Then, and on through his adolescence, he endured surgery after painful surgery on his ankles, hips, and wrists. Even so, his tiny feet droop at odd angles from short, splayed legs. One narrow hand—his right—appears to have been stuck on at a downward ninety-degree angle to his wrist, and the fingers of both are strangely febrile. Ken's face and head might have been designed by Edvard Munch. His tongue rolls awkwardly on its side, part of the reason he has a ferocious stutter.

After the hospital came a series of foster homes. One foster mother loaded Ken and a few other kids into an old station wagon and took off into the mountains of British Columbia in an attempt to escape her alcoholic and abusive husband. More surgeries; after one round, he spent another two years in a hospital until a new foster home could be found.

As soon as he could, Ken moved, on his own, to Toronto. He gets by on minimal government disability support, panhandling when

things are tight, getting food, clothing, and health care from Sanctuary and a few other similar places. He's been beaten for the sake of
the handful of coins in the plastic bucket he ties to the wheelchair,
manipulated and ripped off by a succession of cons who have abused
his generous, eager heart in order to gain access to his apartment or the
tiny income he manages so carefully, and the target of enough cruel
epithets to crush a lesser man.

One crackhead who used to jack him up regularly when he was
panhandling has recently moved into the same building, so Ken is nervous as he waits for the elevator door to open and again when he rolls
out into the lobby. He hasn't had any trouble with the guy since he
moved in, but Ken can't help but feel it's just a matter of time.

Still, there are a high blue sky, a blazing sun, and the whole neighborhood is rockin'. Ken is forty-six today! To him, a birthday means,
first and foremost, that he's still here. Not only has he beat the predic-
tions regarding his mere survival, but he is, against all odds, "living
independently." He lifts his left hand with his right and places it on the
joystick that controls his chair.

Long after leaving his apartment, after hours of rolling through
an endless field of bare, undulating bellies and thighs, jitterbugging in
his chair to the music that pulses everywhere, trying to peek through
the bodies to get a glimpse of the fabulous floats and marching groups
making their way down Yonge Street, Ken arrives at Sanctuary.

Drew has already introduced me to Agnostic Taylor and Pagan
Sabrina. I am giving them the fifty-cent tour, explaining that we consider everything we do here (meals, health care, outreach, employment
training, arts and drama, etc.) to be "church"—worship on Sundays is
just one small though central part.

Because of the Pride parade, all the streets surrounding Sanctuary have been closed to automobile traffic; most of our musicians are missing today. Normally, Dan leads us playing guitar, Shangqui strums along too, Annie plays a washtub bass (yes, an actual washtub bass), John plays electric violin, Sharon and/or Sam handle percussion, one Phil plays drums, and another holds forth on a beautiful Hammond B3 organ, complete with a Leslie speaker, that used to be the house organ at the Apollo Theatre in Brooklyn back in the days of James Brown and Wilson Pickett. It's the closest thing Sanctuary has to a holy relic.

Today it's just me playing piano along with Shangqui, Sam, and John—what with the festivities and crowds outside, a number of our other folks are missing too. It's a bumbling, rambling sort of start to our worship time, but that's not so very unusual. We sing for a bit, songs called out by the people sitting in the horseshoe of chairs that encircles the Communion table. The first tune is the old Curtis Mayfield song "People Get Ready." (A favorite of Pagan Sabrina's, I will learn later.) At one point, as various individuals call the names of the songs they want, sometimes making a comment or a joke (there's lots of laughter), Sabrina leans over and whispers to Taylor, "Do you see how all the power in this ceremony is coming from the people and not the preacher?"

Ken has parked his chair close to the patch of bare wooden floor that serves as a dance floor for various community events; on some of the up-tempo songs, he worships by "dancing" in his chair, tracing circles and figure eights and crazy little squiggles with his head thrown back and his eyes squinched shut. Drew is sitting with his back to a side wall, the brim of his ball cap pulled low.

I invite the group to turn their attention to the Lord's Supper with an informal little liturgy that goes roughly like this:

"This bread reminds us that God knows what it's like to be one of us. He knows what it's like to be hungry, lonely, frustrated, afraid, homeless. He knows what it's like to have his friends turn their backs on him and what it's like to spend time in jail. He knows what it's like to be sad or joyful, to experience victory or defeat, to be loved or despised, to live—and die.

"But he came to do more than just identify with us, or teach us, or show us a better way to live.

"The cup reminds us that he came to die for us, to pour his blood out so that we could be forgiven, cleansed, healed of the sins we've done and the sins we've had done to us. And so that he could welcome us into the family of God—his blood brothers and sisters.

"We don't come to this table because we deserve it or because we've cleaned ourselves up enough, made ourselves good enough. We come because we're hungry and thirsty, starving for Jesus, for God's goodness and grace in our lives.

"Each one of us who takes the bread and wine is saying, 'I believe that Jesus Christ is the Son of the living God, that he died, was buried, and rose again for me.' If you don't believe that, or aren't sure what you believe, don't take it—nobody here will be offended, and we'd much rather you felt free to be honest about where you're at. Regardless of where you find yourself on your spiritual journey, we're glad you're here, and we welcome you in the name of Jesus."

I always encourage our group to pray aloud, read a Scripture, call out another song, or share whatever thoughts they may have that would contribute to our worship—but first, to be silent for a minute or so, so that we can listen for God's voice. Today the silence stretches on. God isn't saying much just yet, I guess. Finally the artist of the imaginary dimension begins to pray. He speaks so quietly it is difficult to hear everything he says, but he leaves an impression of humility, conversational intimacy, and a surprising lucidity. A couple of more songs. Another man prays out loud: He has experienced much fear and isolation in his life because of early life traumas and the psychological conditions they created, but he is grateful for this community where he is welcome and safe, surrounded by brothers and sisters, grateful to know that, because of Jesus, he is accepted by God too.

And Ken prays. His mouth opens wide, wide, stretching his whole face to give the recalcitrant words in his mind every opportunity to make their escape; he pounds his chest with one hand to jolt them free. Sometimes it takes five or ten seconds to get the next word out. The rest of us are concentrating on him, urging the words out of him by the tension in our own necks and jaws, holding in our memories what he said last so that we'll be able to complete it with what he says next. We have a lot of time for Ken—his wheelchair dancing, his complete lack of self-pity, and his appetite for a full, wild, intoxicating relationship with God have won our hearts.

In spite of the stutter, Ken speaks joyfully about his delight in being alive, his gratitude for the good people and things God has given him. Now he is giving thanks for the bread, too. He motors forward across the little dance floor to the Communion table and, parking himself behind it, speaks (equal parts prayer and teaching) about what it meant for Jesus to give his body to be broken for us.

He picks his left wrist up with his right hand, places his left hand on the big glossy challah loaf. His left hand is stronger and more dexterous than his right, but his left arm is significantly weaker. He pauses.

"Can somebody help me?" he asks, looking around. "I can't break it myself."

Someone moves forward, breaks the bread, and holds it so that Ken can tear off a piece for himself. He holds it up in his left hand while his right supports it.

"The body of Christ, broken for us," he says without a hesitation. "Come and eat."

When I check in with Drew after Communion, he is still sitting in the same place with his ball cap on; maybe the brim is a touch lower. He looks a little stunned, and his eyes are wet.

"Hey," I say. "You okay? How are you feeling about all this?"

A little helpless wave of one hand.

"Um. Awkward?"

"Uh-huh."

"I found the silence and lack of 'Church program' painfully awkward. And you! Greg, you're supposed to be the leader of this 'Church,' but I could barely hear you when you actually did decide to say something. I kept waiting for *someone* to move it along. That's what I'm used to, something a little smoother, something a little more leader oriented. I'm not talking about making it a slick operation, but at least a little more professional! I just sat here counting the ugly people …"[3]

He blows his cheeks out soundlessly and squints at me.

"Is it always like this here? Do you have any idea how special this is?"

I laugh and make equivocal noises.

"That first guy who prayed. I saw him outside before. He looked like he was drawing the front of the building. I was going to sit down and talk with him because I love talking to 'different' people, but he kinda creeped me out a bit after I realized that what he was sketching was some apparition of his delusional mind. And then he prays this unbelievably humble, non-look-at-me, contrite prayer…

"And the guy in the wheelchair, Ken … *that* was pretty awkward. All the stuttering and whatnot. I kept waiting for someone to hurry him up. But when he put his shaking hand on the bread and asked for help to break it … man, that's when God found the holy hand grenade up my butt and pulled the pin!"

Drew stares at nothing for a few seconds, then looks back at me.

"I can't remember the last time God showed up in church like that.

"Obviously, the messiness of your socially awkward group of left-overs, especially Ken … well, obviously, this is really where Christ chooses to be. But maybe I'm missing something here. I dunno, I've never met Ken; maybe the guy's the world's biggest jerk."

"No, he's not a jerk," I say. "Anything but. If you knew the rest of his story …"

$ $ $

Mary Wollstonecraft, an eighteenth-century British feminist, wrote in the dedication of *A Vindication of the Rights of Women,* "Independence I have long considered as the grand blessing of life, the basis of every virtue." Certainly the measure of independence Ken has achieved in his difficult life is a "grand blessing." And I desire, for instance, my own children's independence, even though it means my presence in their lives will diminish, because I know it is necessary in order for them to be able to claim their own mature identities.

But a person who lives in complete emotional independence is a sociopath; if he adds to this a total moral independence, he is a psychopath. In short, I think Mary overstated the value of independence. If independence is my destination, or even my exclusive path, mine will be a parched, mean, fierce, friendless, and godless life.

A man like Ken has few illusions about the value or character of independence. He knows on the one hand how precious is the ability to execute for himself the countless daily actions I take for granted; he has discovered, on the other, that the joy of life is found in communion with others whose strengths and weaknesses support and benefit from his own.

Ken and I are teaching each other that independence is best viewed as the base from which we launch out toward our true home. In communion with his "brothers and sisters," Ken finds something of far greater value than the mere ability to do for himself: He discovers the great and deeply fulfilling grace of blessing others. The long, difficult move from being the mere recipient of services offered by professionals and social workers to being able to live with a remarkable degree of independence was not enough. He has come all the way around the circle to a point where he realizes he needs to need other people, not now as service providers, but as brothers and sisters, companions on the journey.

Finding himself in a community where many of those closest to him have enough material wealth and physical health that they have no desire to use him in the ways some of his street connections have so long practiced sets him free to receive the deeper gifts. Now he can experience simple friendship, spiritual intimacy, appreciation of his abilities as, for instance, an artist (yes, he paints!) with no ulterior motive. Among these gifts is the opportunity for him to lead us in worship. There are not many contexts in which a man with Ken's challenges and history would be found literally at the center of the congregation, guiding the people of God in the most potent symbolic observance of our communal lives. The richness Ken derives from this experience enriches all of us.

The presence of Drew and his friends that day was a gift to me, too. His reaction to what he witnessed helped me look with fresh eyes at Ken and others who are part of my communion. (I mean "communion," of course, in a sense that goes far beyond the usual narrow definition having to do with the religious ceremony. Dave, Benny, and Arthur have also been "members" of my "communion," although they've never attended the Sanctuary worship time.) I find it just as easy to grow accustomed to the remarkable spiritual wealth of my friends as it is to forget how truly wealthy I am in material terms.

I took time, a week or so later, to try to tell Ken what he means to me—how he is helping to guide me closer to the heart of God. Ken's physical disabilities are a blatant challenge to my proud self-image as a person of strength and ability—a man who almost always has the resources to help someone else, to *get 'er done*. Not only am I unable to fix anything to do with Ken's body or painful past, but he also turns a mirror on me, revealing all the things I can't fix about myself. I realize that my urge to help others is often rooted in a desire to avoid facing the things *I* need help with; I may even turn away from people because it bruises my ego to discover that their poverty is too deeply entrenched for me to overcome. Ken's tremendous capacity for celebration—his richness as a celebrant of God's grace—reveals to me the miserliness of my own unthankful soul and encourages me to rejoice more deeply in the good things I have; to recognize, in fact, that my own wealth is so abundant that I take absolutely for granted things like hands and legs that work as they should.

I was trying to tell Ken all this in a crowded, noisy drop-in—a hundred hungry, edgy, mostly street-involved people waiting for the food to show up. He listened intently amid the clatter, his eyes searching my face. I had the impression he was thinking, *Yes, I know this already*, but he listened patiently and responded graciously with some words of appreciation for what the Sanctuary community gives to him.

Then he said, "Okay, I have to talk to someone else now," spun his chair around, and began navigating his way through the press of bodies to find another of his companions on the Way.

CHAPTER 8

FROM IMPREGNABILITY TO VULNERABILITY

When we were children, we used to think that when we
were grown-ups we would no longer be vulnerable.
But to grow up is to accept vulnerability.
—*Madeleine L'Engle,* Walking on Water: Reflections on Faith and Art

Your attitude should be the same as that of Christ Jesus:
Who, being in very nature God ...
made himself nothing.
—*Paul, Philippians 2:5–7*

Seven a.m. on an August morning, 1999:

My body leaps from the bed, goosed by an urgent message from some conscious corner of my brain: "They're going to tow the van!"

Residential parking is at a premium in the old, preamalgamation Toronto. The elderly, tall, narrow house we lived in at the time was blessed with a parking pad out front, but I had left it vacant the night before to provide a space for visitors. Unable to find a spot on our own

83

street, I had parked on the main thoroughfare a half block away. Some alarm clock function in my brain has wakened me at precisely the pre-rush-hour moment when city crews begin to tag and tow vehicles without a street parking permit.

As my mind begins to catch up with my body, I am already halfway down the four steep flights of stairs from our third-floor attic bedroom to the main floor. Check: yes, at some point I apparently paused to pull on a pair of shorts. Curious, this gap between my sleep-fogged mind and adrenalin-jacked body. I am through the front door and in the air, leaping the front porch steps. There is the sidewalk below. Oh.

Now I am lying on my side on the concrete. There is a problem, a sensation some wary part of my brain tells me is pain—blood on my knee, a fire farther down that same leg—but now I have bounced up and am sprinting down the street, except it's not a sprint exactly, as I seem to be listing to one side. I am dimly aware of pedestrians watching me curiously as I pass by in this bizarre cork-screwing leaping motion. I have just enough last second awareness to pause for oncoming traffic before crossing Pape Avenue. By the time I reach the van, I am hopping on one leg.

Unlock the van. Fall into the driver's seat. Breathe, finally. No meter maids in sight. No ticket or tow truck. Ha-ha! Beat them! As I start the engine, I feel a fast-growing alarm coming from my left ankle: It's throbbing angrily as if it wants to secede violently from the rest of my body and set up an independent state. There is, I discover, a bulge the size of half a grapefruit on the outside of the ankle. It looks as if it's ready to give birth to a baby ankle, an anklet, or maybe a litter of them.

Later, I will tell whoever is still willing to listen to my whining,

"Next time they can have the van. The air cast alone cost more than impound fees."

I am still a couple of weeks away from being able to get an air cast on it, though. I have ripped the ligaments on both sides of the ankle, and it is much too swollen to get into the rigid plastic boot with adjustable air bladders for support that will eventually seem like such a relief. For now, the tech in the fracture clinic tells me, a half cast of plaster held in place by a lot of soft bandages will have to do. He is not very sympathetic, pointedly telling me about several other people he has treated that week whose ankle bones were vectoring off in several directions at once, even escaping the skin that was supposed to surround them.

Well. My pain is enough for me, is what I say.

By eleven a.m. I am behind my desk at Sanctuary, my foot resting on a pillow with a milk crate beneath it. I am angry and frustrated. The timing sucks.

There are only four of us working full-time at Sanctuary at this juncture, all street outreach workers—no administrative staff, no "development" department—and we have three and a half months to find half-a-million dollars to buy the building that has become home to our mostly homeless community over the past seven years—or lose it. We can't afford professional fund-raisers and have no real fund-raising experience ourselves. It would take the "congregation" significantly longer than we have to panhandle that amount. With no other options, I have taken most of this responsibility on myself, so that the other staff members can continue to care well for our people.

A week before, I had arrived at Sanctuary, placed my backpack on the steps, and unlocked the door. In the time it took to get my bicycle inside, prop it against the wall, turn the security alarm off, and open the door again, someone stole my backpack. It contained my laptop and all my hard-copy files for our seat-of-the-pants fund-raising campaign—all the names and contact information for all the people who might be able to help us, notes about what contacts had been made, dates and locations for meetings that were upcoming. Whatever backup files I had (precious few) were also in the backpack, along with my glasses and several other difficult-to-replace personal items.

A week from now, it will get a little worse. Climbing the stairs, a crutch will slip, and I will boot the riser with my clumsy left foot in its ridiculous half cast and bandages. My leg is already swollen so that it is a smooth, straight column from calf to foot, but new swelling on the front half of the foot and, the next morning, purple and green toes tell me what an X-ray will later confirm: a broken bone in the middle of my foot.

I am, by this point, feeling sorry for myself. A gnawing fear: *What if we can't find the money?*

Most of my friends on the street think the whole leg debacle is hilarious. When I first show up with this big fluffy white confection on my leg, members of the Brew Crew laugh out loud, pointing at it, har har har, calling others of their mates over to see. Gashes, bruises, broken bones, and lost teeth are practically a daily occurrence for Marty, Randy, Glenda, Lenny, April, Frank, the Colonel, and Brian.

"A little too much wobbly pop last night, Padre?" Lenny crows. "Haw, haw."

The winter before, one of them—Randy, I think, or maybe Lenny—had leaned back, the better to empty a tall can of strong beer, and discovered too late that there was no back to lean against on the concrete abutment on which he was perched. He tumbled down its side, bonking his melon several times before landing in the Don River below. The rest of them scrambled down the embankment to help him out, but since they were all pretty stinko, a couple more landed in the icy water. It took them half an hour to get everybody out and who knows how long to get dry and warm. Bruises, concussion, and incipient pneumonia. It was all good fun to them.[1]

When I told them how my injury had occurred, and why, they thought it was funnier still. The image of me blindly leaping down the stairs in my boxers, collapsing in a heap on the sidewalk, then pogoing down the street with one swollen ankle tucked up behind me was endlessly satisfying. They wiped their eyes and insisted on writing messages on my cast, some touching and some obscene. Then they laughed some more.

I quickly tired of telling the true story—I had literally hundreds of people asking me what I had done to myself, and was it catching? I enjoyed the camaraderie of laughing about it with the Brew Crew, but underneath I was still cranky about the timing of it—I had so much to do! I grew weary of trying to explain the trials of parking safely and living in a multistory house to inquirers, who often had nowhere to live, and certainly nothing to park, and so I concocted a new, concise, and less-humiliating story.

I told people I had jumped from a burning building with a child in my arms.

As intended, most of my friends responded with a laugh and, "No, really, what happened?" But some, to my surprise, nodded their heads seriously and said, "No, really? Wow."

It gave me pause. I began to realize that I had so successfully projected a particular image of myself that jumping from a building with a child in my arms was precisely the kind of thing certain more gullible members of our community expected I would do. As far as they were concerned, I *was* bulletproof, able to clear at least low buildings with a single bound. The thought that I might not be able to successfully clear my own porch steps never occurred to them. When I quickly backpedaled, explaining that the child-from-the-burning-house story was just a joke, they looked puzzled, disappointed. And even more so when I told them what had really happened.

$ $ $

Dave is standing ten feet away from me, his shirt hanging open, toweling his wet hair. It's early in the drop-in, so the place isn't crowded yet, but he has already had a shower and is staking out his seat at one of the tables before the lunch rush floods the place. There are old bleary tattoos on his chest that leap as he rubs his head, and more on his arms.

I am perched with my butt on the back of a couch, watching him and cogitating, as I often do, on one of the deeper mysteries of life: How is it that Dave, who is ten years older than I, and has abused himself mercilessly for almost his entire adult life, who eats and wears whatever he can scrounge, and has been sleeping outside for at least a decade, has a full head of glossy hair, while I—who eat and drink mostly healthy stuff, in moderate amounts, and ride my bike and play a little hockey to stay in shape, and generally get enough sleep in a safe, dry bed—am left with only paltry gray stubble? This, I believe, is evidence that the whole of the cosmos fell along with Adam and Eve; that it is still a sick, broken, sinful world; that "judgment is turned away backward, and justice standeth afar off: for truth is fallen in the street, and equity cannot enter" (Isa. 59:14 KJV).[2]

When I surface from my little reverie, Dave is standing, regarding me with steady blue eyes, his head cocked a bit, his fists hanging from the ends of the towel now draped around his neck.

"Are you okay?" he asks.

"Yep." My response is quick, automatic. "You?"

Dave just nods slowly, pursing his lips, and sits down.

The drop-in fills up, things get busy, the food is served. But I find myself thinking about Dave, his question, and his story—a story he has, through the years and with great generosity, shared with me.

It's an incredible tale and worth a book of its own. Dave is working on writing his story down, but I'll sketch out just a little of it here.

He was adopted as an infant, but his new family had difficulties too. Dave spent a lot of time being shuttled between various relatives. The good part of that was spending summers at Aunt Alma's cottage by the lake in northern Ontario, swimming, fishing, paddling around in an old canoe. Watching a pine fire pop and hiss on the little rocky point at night, or lying on the dock, looking at the stars, and listening to the heartrending calls of the loons and whip-poor-wills.

There wasn't much else to keep him, though. At eighteen he crossed the border at Buffalo and signed up for the U.S. Army. Because he displayed a talent for long-range shooting and general mayhem, and above all because he was Canadian and therefore more easily deniable, he was streamed into a CIA-run black ops unit that had been labeled the Phoenix Program. Dave and the other members of his team were nullifying certain preidentified liabilities in neutral territory, and doing so with extreme prejudice, even as President Nixon was proclaiming that "there are no American troops in Cambodia" with an indignant waggle of his jowls.

It was a surreal, incendiary world, fueled by fear, testosterone, and exotic drugs. (I went to see *Apocalypse Now* with him when the *Redux* version came out. During the scene in which Martin Sheen finds himself in the middle of a firefight, among acid-stoned soldiers who are listening to Jimi Hendrix and have no idea who they are fighting or who is in charge of their own unit, Dave declared several times, "I was there! I was there!")

His group was cut off and left for dead at one point, and the handful who survived initially, Dave included, spent the next year and a half in the bamboo cages and deep, soggy-bottomed pits that constituted a Viet Cong prison camp. They escaped, eventually, by dragging a guard into the pit with them. Seizing the camp's open channel radio, they called in an air strike and headed for the jungle to wait for the chopper that would eventually pick them up.

They were delivered to a nearby Aussie special forces base, which seemed a little strange at the time. Stranger still, but barely a cause for shock after all they had been through, was the explosion that sent the helicopter pin-tailing into the jungle just minutes after it had dropped them off. When they finally made it back stateside, by inexplicably convoluted routes, they found they had long since been posted KIA. The nature of their mission had all along been unavowed, of course; they were an embarrassment to the government and underwent extensive "debriefing" to ensure that their story would not become public.

Months later, Dave rang the doorbell of his father's house. His father opened the door, saw the ghost of his son, and promptly had a heart attack. Dave maintains to this day that his real name is listed on the long black wall of the Vietnam Memorial in Washington, D.C.

Most vets find it difficult to transition back into "normal" life, especially when they've seen the kind of extreme engagement Dave had. Entire villages disappearing in a great, sucking whoosh of napalm—the oily stink and small blazing comets of it still raining from the sky hours later. A helicopter blown out of the air by a bomb hidden in the corpse of a baby handed off to corpsmen at the last second by its Viet Cong "mother." Mates and enemies shrieking out their last breaths, their bodies turned inside out by land mines or the tumbling shells of an AK-47. A head in the crosshairs of a telescopic sight, whole one moment and a soundless explosion of red mush the next. A rat plucked from the wall of the pit and, for the first time, not merely killed and thrown clear, but its pelt ripped off and eaten like a cob of corn.

Dave never did make the transition back home. He ran guns and drugs for an outlaw biker club, did some other dirty work for them and, occasionally, for one or two of the shadowy characters who used to show up with assignments at the camp in Cambodia. He did a few banks and, once, an armored truck. He did some pen time. He lived in a town in his beloved north country for a few years, the most nearly normal period of his adult life, keeping his head down and learning to do taxidermy. Later on he lived in a western city, helping an old pal run an armaments business. A deal went bad; he let the yokels who came to get him enter his darkened house before he kneecapped them. That was good for a federal warrant, and with his record he knew he'd be given a long, long stretch. It was time to go to ground in a serious way.

That's how he ended up on the streets in Toronto. It's easy to get

lost here. Since the early nineties he's been haunting the ravines and
alleyways, sleeping in doorways, under bridges, in cemeteries, and,
lately, beneath a concrete abutment to one side of an apartment building just a five-minute walk from where I sit writing this. For a time,
he'd sleep in good weather on top of a large domed rock in the middle
of Yorkville, where the glitterati come to play when they're in Toronto.
He's been given money or told to beat it by most of the movie stars you
might think of.

Dave has been lost in more ways than one. Getting by, just keeping his head down—chasing the dragon, as they say, to help keep the
boredom or the pain or the memories at bay.

And now, here in the drop-in, I'm thinking of all that Dave has
told me about himself through these many years, making himself vulnerable in ways that are extraordinarily risky, trusting *me* in a way and
to a degree that is courageous for him and humbling for me. Watching
him silently eat his pork chops, forearms on the table and head bent
over his plate, I think of how he spent Christmas morning at our house
the year before last, enjoying the huge brunch Karen had prepared,
opening the little gifts we had got him, and watching with quiet pleasure as the kids opened theirs. Dozing on the couch with his jaw on his
chest and his face obscured by a shaggy curtain of hair.

I know that, although he would not likely ever use the word, he
loves Karen and he loves me. He knows me well enough to be able to
tell just by looking at me that I'm not okay. I'm ashamed that I have
so quickly brushed aside his gentle inquiry. So when the drop-in has
cleared a bit, I go to him, sit beside him, and confess.

Things are not okay. I am not okay, and I'm sorry I avoided his
concern like that. The deep, dark truth is that my marriage has come

apart; it seems unlikely Karen and I will survive as a couple. I don't know that things have ever been worse. It doesn't take a lot of time; I don't offer much detail, and Dave doesn't ask. I'm as honest as I know how to be about how crummy, how desperate and desperately sad I feel about myself and the whole situation. Dave listens gravely. He is not surprised. He could see this, sense it in us. He doesn't tell me that he knows how I feel or that it will be okay. He hears everything I say and, I'm convinced, so much that I do not.

$ $ $

When I sit down kitty-corner to him and say hello, Sheldon pins a hard, cold glare on me. He used to be tall and lean, rough and ropy as a twist of rawhide, a fearsome boy on the streets. Now he's a long bundle of dry sticks, teeth rotted to black stubs beneath a red, swollen, deeply pitted nose. Hanks of long, matted black hair bound by a bandana. A deep hollow between tendon and bone where the neck of his T-shirt is stretched to a yawning, lopsided O.

When I ask him how he's doing, he continues to stare at me for another long moment before beginning a careful, thorough description of the actions (mostly impossible, all obscene) he thinks I should perform on myself, interspersed with reflections on my character and origins. I listen until he's done, then respond in kind, although I cannot match his inventiveness, his verve, his bold command of the vernacular. When we're both done, we sit there looking at each other, grim as a couple of Highland cliffs.

"You're smiling," I say finally, although he is not.

A little grin flickers at the corner of his mouth, works its way across. He laughs, an almost soundless creak, and reaches for my hand.

Sheldon is an old friend. He is full-blooded Blackfoot, born on the rez in the foothills of Alberta, but raised everywhere: foster homes, distant relatives, juvenile detention center. Later, he was in a penitentiary on a manslaughter charge—the other guy started the argument, but Sheldon finished it. He spent time in fishing villages on the west coast, prairie towns, and, for these past many years now, Toronto. Alleys, the little parks, sometimes a week or so in summer out on the Leslie Spit, or avoiding the parks people on the Toronto Islands. There are birds there, and water, and more sky than the narrow ribbon that wanders between the heads of the buildings along Yonge Street, Bay Street, Spadina Avenue.

It's amazing to me that Sheldon and I are friends. It speaks far more to his graciousness than mine. I am white, wealthy, and Christian—most of what he and his people have suffered has been as a result of the actions of people just like me. We have shoved native people onto tracts of land not useful to us (except in some cases where the usefulness of oil, for example, or electricity or lumber became apparent only much later), focused the energy of church and state on eradicating their culture, taken and abused their children under the guise of educating or converting them; and now we throw money at them to keep them tame.

So there is a very real, deeply rooted, and largely justified anger at the heart of the verbal "abuse" Sheldon often lays on me when we meet. When he pretends, at first, not to know me, it is more than just a joke. There is a wide, swift river of pain and resentment he must cross to be able to take my hand as friend and brother. He doesn't pretend it isn't there. But he does cross it.

Sheldon has been an alcoholic for a long time now. Although he is more or less sober today, I can smell the Listerine on him. Strange that a product intended to make your breath smell fresh gives such a distinctive, sour tang to a person's sweat. If, as happens only rarely, Sheldon goes twelve or eighteen hours without a drink, he will begin to have seizures. Withdrawal from heroin can make a person sick for a couple of weeks. Cold turkey withdrawal from an addiction to alcohol, like Sheldon's, can be lethal. I have lost friends that way before. And I know that Sheldon has been coughing up blood for an absurdly long time—perhaps a couple of years.

When I ask him how he's doing, it's not merely a polite convention. I want to know. He tells me without melodrama or a hint of self-pity, but I know that he has been suffering so much for so long and that he keeps himself so anesthetized that the pains and bodily malfunctions he describes matter-of-factly would send me or any of my ilk screaming and panic-stricken to the doctor. It's a matter of some wonder to me that he is alive at all.

And he asks me how I'm doing, too.

I may be a slow, reluctant traveler, but Dave and others have led me far enough along this journey that I am ready to tell him the truth. If my boat was listing badly when I talked to Dave, by now it has had so many holes blown in it that it's in imminent danger of sinking. The Sanctuary board has mandated two months of sabbatical—much more if I need it. I am not here today to function as a staff person, helping to facilitate the drop-in. I'm here because this is where many of my friends are. I have come today specifically because I need their care and support. (It's a testament to the journey our board members have been on that they understand and affirm this. In many other places, where the people coming through the door are seen as clients, I would have been required to remove myself entirely, on the assumption that their needs could only be a further drain: The idea that *they* might look after *me* would be unthinkable.)

Sheldon listens quietly. His eyes lock on mine as I tell him that my father, previously as healthy and vital as most men twenty years his junior, died recently as a result of a freak accident. That we had stood around his bed, watching and praying for three days, before making the necessary yet impossible decision to remove the life supports. That the day before the accident, Karen and I had separated; that a few days before that, we had had the impossible yet necessary discussion with our children. I continue, hoping that I am being as restrained and dignified as he was, telling him that the family dog, a stray that had followed my eldest son, Caleb, home ten years ago, died a week or two after my dad.

I laugh and say that it's beginning to feel like I'm living in a country-and-western song. Sheldon smiles, but the smile dies quickly, and his eyes do not leave my face. We buried Herbie—overdose—a few weeks ago, and I just heard that Hello Hello Larry, another street pal, died the other day as a result of a beating. So that's how I'm doing.

Like Dave, Sheldon doesn't say a lot. He doesn't have to. His eyes, the stillness of his bloated features, the pressure of his hand on mine speak louder than his soft words.

Sheldon is called away—the nurse is ready to see him. Keren Elumir and Thea Prescod, our nurses, never discuss with the rest of us the nature of a patient's confidential medical concerns, but Keren will tell me a day or so later about the last few minutes of Sheldon's visit to the clinic.

While Sheldon has only harsh or cynical words to say about the "white man's god" in public, he is, like most of my native friends, deeply aware of the Creator and his presence in the world around him. When Keren is done addressing Sheldon's medical needs, she asks him, as she often does, if she can pray for him. The clinic functions for some as a kind of Holy of Holies, an inner sanctum of security and confidentiality where considerations, admissions, and confessions that would never be broached elsewhere may be entertained. On this day, however, Sheldon does not simply say "yes" and bow his head as usual.

"I tell you what," he says pensively, still sitting in the chair. He pats the hand she has placed on his shoulder, peers up at her. "You save that prayer for Greg. He really needs it right now—more than me."

$ $ $

If independence is the way I glory in my wealth and power, then my desire for impregnability is the way I try to protect my many faults, weaknesses, and insecurities from being revealed and exploited. I run faster, jump higher, work harder to prove to myself and to others and maybe even to God that I'm okay.

The impregnability of my poor friends, although the same in essence, looks different. Some have so abandoned personal pride that there is virtually nothing that could be done to them that could diminish their dignity any further. These are men and women who would perform almost any criminal, sexual, or violent act, abasing themselves or someone else in order to feel, if just for a few minutes, the euphoric inviolability of a crack high. Some would drink anything with alcohol in it until they are so numb that nothing can pierce them. "You can't hurt me," they say, in effect, "because I can't feel you."

Some have built invisible fortresses around them by opting out of conventional society, leaving behind homes, families, careers, and government lists, in effect becoming hermits in the very midst of millions of people. I have one good friend who has developed an amazing capacity to "disappear" in a roomful of people. He will stand in a corner with his head down, arms limp, utterly motionless for hours at a time, as if someone had turned him off and gone home. I have seen him do the same thing in the middle of winter at the edge of the little park next door to Sanctuary. You would take no more particular notice of him than you would of one of the trees. It's a kind of camouflage. He is an older man and not physically strong; this is how he avoids the potentially violent confrontations that are so common in the street community. "You can't hurt me, because I'm not really here."

Others build their fortresses out of reputations for ruthlessness, violence, cold, cynical amorality. Defending a small patch of sidewalk like *mujahideen* defending the honor of Muhammad. "You can't touch me, because I don't care about myself. Or anyone else."

For those who believed the image I projected of impregnability, the very thing about me they respected became an impediment to deeper relationship. My "wealthy" friends readily commiserated with my frustration and physical discomfort, but their own self-sufficiency never challenged my ego-driven need to hide behind the fiction of myself as immovable object.

Some of my friends, both rich and poor, want to believe in my impregnability as much as I do—they want an icon, someone utterly dependable, someone who will never disappoint or let them down. Even just believing that someone somewhere could be that is a powerful, seductive fantasy. It's how cults are born.

It was the familiarity of the Brew Crew with foolish, humbling, unnecessary injuries that slipped past my defenses, allowed me to laugh at myself. It was the destruction of the fiction of my impregnability that allowed us a degree of intimacy and tender care that we hadn't had before. When I let Dave take care of me, it brought about a new depth in our relationship and a new measure of health in my life and his. The Brew Crew and Dave guided me far enough along the road that I was ready to be open with Sheldon and so receive the blessing he offered.

I can't honestly say how much of an impact this had on their journeys, but I do know that catching a glimpse of my weakness makes me more approachable to my friends—any friends from any kind of society—than endless evidence of my "invulnerability." It opens me up to receive the care my bristling heart truly needs but often keeps at a distance. Dismantling that myth is, for me, like breaking down the walls of a prison I had built for myself, setting me free to step out on the Way again—that Way which is itself the One who made himself so gloriously, dangerously vulnerable on the cross. Each step is a step deeper into the land where love dwells.

FROM PRODUCTIVITY TO FRUITFULNESS

*I am the vine; you are the branches. Whoever abides in me
and I in him, he it is that bears much fruit.*
—*Jesus, John 15:5* ESV

MANDY

A middle-aged sedan rolls to a stop where she stands teetering on the curb with both hands demurely clutching a tiny white purse. (The older girls tell her she should make a point of remembering make, model, color—license number, too, if possible. She makes a point of noticing as little as possible and forgetting what she can.) It's beyond frigid, and there's little traffic this late on a dark side street, but even here the pristine layer that is still thickening one fat, drifting flake at a time will be pummeled to gray slush by midmorning. There's a border of frost on the passenger window. It's mostly steamed up: *He's been driving around, breathing heavy for an hour,* she thinks. A little internal snort of derision. At least an hour. She saw him drive past once or twice that long ago, just before she broke last. Maybe he was waiting for her to return.

In the moment before the window hums down into the door, she sees reflected what brought him round again: a slender, pale little girl, her hair gathered into a childish blond spout on top of her head. A pouty rosebud of lips, purpled by the cold. Bright, round blue eyes, dimpled cheeks, tiny pink ears with a teddy bear stud in each one.

Beneath the face of innocent childhood is a small but perfectly proportioned woman's body, swelling with surprising generosity in all the right places. A short shell pink jacket with a fur-trimmed hood, unzipped in spite of the brittle air, revealing a tight, light, low-necked sweater beneath. Jaunty little suede boots with spike heels. Between the boots and jacket, bare legs, goose-pimpled and blue, rising into the inference of a skirt.

She does not stifle a shiver, knowing it will add to the overall effect. The driver has popped the lock, is leaning across the big bench seat to invite her in. She leans through the window instead, giving him a closer look, wafting mascara-clotted eyelashes at him, wiggling her upper body—ooo, it's cold out here—all obvious, shameless, because of course the fiction they're both working on is that she doesn't really know what she's doing.

A bit of suggestive banter, smiles on each side. He invites her in out of the cold again. She slithers her way back out of the window, swings the door open, and slips inside. The rising window catches a lock of her hair because she has planted her back against the door; a squeak of pain from her, profuse apologies, and a lunging attempt to set her free from him. She pouts a bit, pretending to be hurt more than she actually is.

She should have agreed on a specific service and price before getting in the car. That's the accepted way, the safer way. She never does though, believing she can ratchet the price higher by playing on her apparent naïveté. It's backward from the way the other girls do it and pleases her to know that, same as it does when she deliberately doesn't try to remember the details about the car or even the john himself. She takes risks others won't, makes deals other don't, works purely on instinct. Even then, sometimes some fierce, dark thing rises in her and drives her past those parts of her mind that are screaming, *"No!"*

And this one will be trouble, although she's not sure why she thinks that. He looks and acts normal enough. What she is sure of is that she can take him—take him and his money, wiggle out of whatever dumb or dangerous little arrangement he has planned, and be back to the hotel room where Toko and the rest are holed up within half an hour. With the proceeds of three dates in less than three hours—more money than the rest of them will have made put together, after a long day of panhandling, boosting and selling stuff, or hustling their skanky little butts for coffee money over on Isabella or down in Boystown. She can do it at any time of any day or night. The other girls admire and hate her for it; the guys are always on the verge of fighting each other over who's going to get next to her. In their world, there's nothing hotter than a cute girl who can make a mittful of cash anytime she wants.

She plays the john a bit, getting him to talk about what he wants, pretending to be a little shocked but excited too—*won't that be fun; never done anything like that before!*—waiting until she can see that he's starting to get worked up before slipping smoothly out of little-girl mode to name a price. He nods, doesn't even flinch. A mouth breather. She could have asked for more. She tells him she needs the money first; he lifts one cheek and starts hauling his wallet awkwardly out of his back pocket before she's finished talking. She takes the cash bashfully—a little girl again—and tucks it into her purse, among the five rolls of pennies she keeps there at all times. Then, as he hoists himself to replace the wallet, she moves close to him, breathing heavy and stroking his thigh. He stuffs the wallet in his jacket pocket instead. Mission accomplished.

Around the block to an even darker alley. She waits in the front while he moves the child's car seat from the back, puts it in the trunk. Then she launches herself over the backrest with a wild giggle. Strips quickly—her clothing calculated for this—while he watches, trying to be cool. Drapes her stuff carefully over the back of the front seat, coaxes him out of his jacket, and places it on top. Her purse in one hand or the other at all times.

She positions herself as he directs, makes the requisite movements and noises. Waiting for the wrinkle she's sure he will throw into it.

And here it is: He is behind her, swearing steadily and without imagination—and now his hands are around her throat. Big hands, small throat. Amazing how quickly an inky darkness floods the perimeter of her vision. A tide of something similarly dark but fiery flooding her core. Even later she will not be able to tell if it is fear or excitement.

She drops facedown on the vinyl seat, kicks up and back as hard as she can into his torso with first one spike heel, then the other, then both together. He swears louder, a yelp, but his hands loosen and the darkness recedes. She kicks him again, then writhes around, and slams her purse against the side of his head. The rolled up pennies go *thunk!* and he sags to the side. She whacks him twice more, wiggles out from beneath him as he begins to slump. Once more with the deadly little purse, this time with two hands and everything she can put into it, given the confined space. She is on her back on the floor now, wedged into the small carpeted well between the bench of the back seat and the backrest of the front seat. One foot is still tangled beneath his legs, but the rest of her is free. He is flopped chest down on the seat, his face turned toward her. Eyes fluttering. Moaning, a purple goose egg already rising from his right temple.

He is badly dazed, but not really unconscious and won't be long coming around. She kicks her foot free of him—later she will think with wicked pleasure of him trying to explain the mess on the side of his head and the scattering of small, round, livid bruises on his torso and thigh to the mother of the child whose seat he had so hurriedly placed in the trunk. Reaching above and behind her, she unlatches the car door, pushes it wide open. Sits up, backs out of the car, grabs her clothing and his jacket. Whacks the bruised side of his head with the purse once more, slams the door, and runs deeper into the alley as she pulls his jacket on. It's so big on her it fits like an oversized dress.

Behind a Dumpster, she sheds the jacket, dresses in her own clothing, and puts the jacket back on over it all. It's new, a brand she knows Toko favors. At the deepest, darkest end of this alley is a narrow defile between one building and another; a slender girl can run easily through it, but not so a large man. At the far end of it, Mandy steps back into the comparatively bright lights of Jarvis Street. She takes the wallet from the pocket of the jacket, thumbs through the cash and cards. She laughs out loud, an explosion of relief and excitement.

She imagines, ten minutes from now, Toko responding to her knock on the hotel room door. The look on his face when she hands him a new FUBU jacket. The glee, the sullen respect on the other faces when she piles the product of her night's labors on the corner of one of the beds—*Mandy's done it again!*

And she laughs again, her whole body shaking.

SUSAN

Here is Susan, dusting the furniture in the living room of her comfortable-but-not-extravagant Don Mills back-split. Note how calmly efficient she is, movements economical but effective, working highest to lowest: the valance over the bow window, the mantelpiece, the side tables, the coffee table. She likes to keep busy and has never seriously considered hiring a maid service, unlike most of her peers. Next she will vacuum, then she will scrub the kitchen from stem to stern. Listen to her hum a quiet melody as she works, steady and serene ...

But the melody falters periodically, and she finds herself self-consciously taking it up again, a kind of shield against the roiling panic at the perimeter of her interior vision. Cleaning the house is a weekend ritual—Saturday afternoons, usually, since the morning is generally taken up by work she has brought home, and Sunday is for church, family, and friends. She lives alone, and never leaves a mess behind her, even during the stress of the workweek, so the cleaning required is minimal. The scouring she is subjecting the house to today, up at dawn, still going strong at four in the afternoon, is largely unnecessary.

She knows this. She watches her hands as one lifts the center-piece on the dining room table and the other wipes beneath it. Odd. Some disconnected part of her observes everything she does. Susan, a flier-under-the-radar if ever there was one, is at this critical moment offering a bravura performance in a theater where the sum of the actors and audience is one.

She smiles to herself at the idea—actually smiles; that's good.

"You can take the weekend to think about it," Parker had said. With down-turned eyes. A swat of his hand, meant, probably, to be expansive, but coming across as dismissive. Shoo, fly.

But Susan, so adept at assessing, recording, and reconciling debits and credits, whose cool-but-not-uncompassionate resources have been tapped by others in many a financial or emotional recession, finds she is struggling to balance this particular account. She knows all the relevant figures, but they will not stay in their proper columns.

Parker has presented her with three possible bottom lines. Parker Henderson, who enters every room chin first. Parker Henderson, who, now that he is the newest member of the national senior executive team, no longer parts his hair severely on the side in a bid to look older and more responsible. Now it suits him to have it professionally tousled and lacquered, for he is young, buoyant, aggressive—the face of Karu's corporate future. Today he is CFO; tomorrow he will be King.

"As the company grows, Susan, the controller will naturally become my successor."

When the Glorious Day arrives, and I ascend to the Throne, I must have loyal lackeys who will rise with me.

"You've done a fabulous job for us for a long time—what, twenty-plus years? Really? Twenty-six? Wow. At any rate, in the judgment of the senior exec," he said, gazing carefully over her shoulder at the field of cubicles beyond this fishbowl of a board room, "you're not the right person to become CFO. So that's why we have to replace you as controller ..."

You have been around much longer than I, know more about how the company actually works than I. The accounting staff are fiercely loyal to you because you have for so long been fiercely loyal to them. Besides, you are steady and competent and dedicated, not young or buoyant or aggressive ...

Parker raised a hand to run it through his hair, a most un-Parker-like gesture, a measure of his discomfiture, but remembered his new coiffure at the last second and passed it instead an inch above the stiff little peaks as if blessing himself. Susan was looking right at him, but he could not meet her eyes. Never did throughout the whole conversation.

She had been angry about that at the time, but remembering it now (as she changes the bag on the vacuum cleaner), she tells herself to give him a break. Make some kind of effort to be Christlike. Probably he did feel badly about having to ax a quarter-century company servant—she had certainly never seen him look and act less confident—and these things, these days, are rarely personal. Often a firing is not even a comment on the victim's competence or lack thereof; one does not rise to be a key member of the senior management team of a corporation like Karu without being very good at one's job. It's just the politics of business.

Susan clicks off the vacuum cleaner, drops the wand in the middle of the hallway. She walks to the living room and plunks herself down in an armchair facing the window. The bright, bitter-cold winter afternoon is dying into a charcoal night, punctured by the orange glow of the streetlight at the end of her driveway. She suddenly realizes it has gotten quite dark in the house—how has she been able to see what she's been vacuuming?—and reaches over to turn on a floor lamp.

So, the three options.

"You can, of course, choose to leave immediately, and we'll work out a package."

That package, Susan thinks as she stares absently at the shadow of herself slumped in the chair, now dimly reflected in the window, should be pretty substantial. A whack of cash, company stocks that have—a flash of pride—been steadily rising for twenty years.

"Or you can stay on as controller until the end of June, and leave then, again, of course, with a package."

Of course.

"Or, if you want to stay on after the end of June, we'll find another position for you." Parker cleared his throat and blessed himself again. "But you won't be controller."

Of course not. *We'll find some closet to stick you in. Move you around, sideways and slowly downward, always outward, until you get fed up and quit.*

A dart of insight: Parker assumes that she will take option two. In fact, he's banking on it. He assumes, because he knows firsthand her deep commitment to and regular defense of the staff of the accounting department—virtually all of whom she has hired and trained herself. "Susan's Brood," she has heard them called. He believes she will not be able to abandon them so quickly—that, in fact, she will feel like leaving immediately *is* a kind of abandonment. And he's banking on it because he doesn't yet have anyone in place to take over—the six-month option wouldn't have been offered, otherwise—and he wants it to ultimately appear that she has left of her own accord so that her staff doesn't engage in silent revolt. Parker knows that she has built a top-notch department, and while he doesn't want her, he does want it intact. Option three is no option at all, and both of them know it. He might as well have offered to replace her computers with a mop and pail.

She should have seen it coming. A new CEO after a generation of unchanged leadership—which had therefore grown a little fusty, some said, but old George was the guy who had planted an acorn and grown it into a mighty oak before retiring on his own timetable, virtually unchallenged. A new mantra and solemn warning: "If this team can't meet those goals, we'll find one that will."

A moment, here, of sickening self-doubt for Susan. (Up and moving again: filling the kitchen sink with hot soapy water, depositing the burner grills from the gas stove therein to soak while she scrubs the pans beneath.) *Have I been sacked because they thought I couldn't deliver?* But a moment only, really. She knows what she has done over the past twenty-six years, remembers the reverence with which old George treated her. No, she has been productive and then some. She never had to play office politics because her work was unassailable. But now.

Suddenly, she knows what she will do—which of Parker's three options she will take. Such an uncharacteristically emotional certainty that she leaves off cleaning and deliberately goes about doing her due diligence anyway, phoning colleagues, peers, friends, her father (his near apoplectic reaction to the news of her termination not practically helpful with the decision-making process, but immensely gratifying nonetheless), creating a handwritten ledger of pros and cons. Praying, of course. (This Father has as little helpful advice to offer as her earthly one, but seems to express, though without the sputtering, a similar conviction regarding her own enduring value and that simple commitment to walk with her through whatever waters may rise, which she has come to view as priceless.)

She does, as Parker foresaw, struggle with the thought of leaving her brood defenseless with the night coming on and the wolves howling in the hills. But she finds herself smiling, even as she dutifully records the opinions of her advisers (phone wedged between shoulder and cheek) and fiddles with the relative values of the items on the ledger, at how surprised Parker will be.

He'll look at her in disbelief and more than a little panic. He'll fuss a bit, and she'll have to remind him, "That *was* Option One, Parker ..." He'll throw up his hands—literally, he's a hand talker—and relinquish her to the tender care of the HR department.

And that. Will. Be. That.

Her brood will weather the storm. Only a fool would dismantle or upset a department that solid and efficient, and Parker is not a fool. They will face adjusting to a new corporate environment and a new leader less tuned to their individual strengths and weaknesses, but they will have to do so either now or in six months, regardless of what Susan does. And leaving this way will let them know, without speaking a word, that she did not go of her own will, that her care for them through these years was not fiction, a tap she could turn off and walk away from. She knows these things are true, even though she also knows she will second-guess her decision for weeks.

Perhaps, given the settlement she will begin negotiating with them on Monday, this will be a time to take less-demanding work, maybe contracts or consultancy. (Amazing how quickly Karu, which only yesterday was "us," has become "them.") Her needs are simple—no dependents, the house long since mortgage free—maybe she'll just work for free for two or three charities she cares about.

Since recognizing the discomfited look Parker wore when she sat down at the board table yesterday afternoon (she's worn it herself on many a similar occasion), she has been mostly numb, although, truth to tell, there has also been the odd stomach-clutching wave of anger or panic. Now, as she folds back the duvet on her bed, she feels ... not exactly happy, or even content, but at peace. She climbs beneath the covers and turns out the light.

Three hours later, she wakens suddenly, completely. Blank darkness in her room. Silence. A weight like a stone upon her chest.

Who am I now, then? I was Susan, controller of Karu International ...

CHAPTER 9

PRODUCTIVITY AND FRUITFULNESS

We have created an industrial order geared to automatism, where feeble-mindedness, native or acquired, is necessary for docile productivity in the factory; and where a pervasive neurosis is the final gift of the meaningless life that issues forth at the other end.
—*Lewis Mumford,* The Conduct of Life

I am the vine; you are the branches. If a man remains in me and I in him, he will bear much fruit; apart from me you can do nothing.
—*Jesus, John 15:5*

"Treating depressed workers boosts productivity, retention: study" said the headline of an article I read online recently. The opening paragraph went on to summarize an article in the *Journal of the American Medical Association*: "Taking care of depressed employees through screening and enhanced-care programs may be beneficial to employers, finds a new study."[1]

I wondered, as I read it, how much the suspicion that the value of their lives could be assessed by their capacity to produce the highest possible number of widgets with the fewest possible resources contributed to the depression of the workers in the study. And if their treatment would be adversely affected if they dwelled too long on the notion that their employers' "enhanced care" for them was motivated by the same mantra of "output created per unit input used." After all, retaining employees is cheaper than training new ones.

We're not machines. We're living, breathing, growing, creating beings, created in love by the Father, each of us unique down to the very DNA strands that (so I'm told) are the basic unit of our biological selves, the highly mutable and continually evolving sum of the incredible range of experiences that have shaped each one of us from the very moment of conception onward. We long for that uniqueness to be recognized and valued. We want to know that we *matter*.

In this sense, we want to be productive—to know that we have something to offer, the ability to do or create things that other people want. Most of us desire this, not just to stroke our egos or make ourselves more comfortable, but because we are also possessed with an urge to bless or benefit others, according to our own gifts. It's one of the ways we display the hallmark of our Creator, who said, "Let us make mankind in our image, after our likeness" (Gen. 1:26).

But productivity as an end in itself—the kind of productivity our Western society has made into a religion—comes at an exorbitant human cost. Our insatiable appetite for the best product at the lowest price has made virtual slaves of a couple of billion people in third world nations. That's a matter that deserves a library or two of books to itself, but my purpose is more modest, and perhaps more selfish: it's diminishing us here in the first world, too.

The Corporation,[2] a 2003 documentary that has won numerous awards, points out that corporations are as pervasive a presence in our culture as was the church in centuries gone by.[3] It goes on to observe, chillingly, that corporations have the status of persons by law, but persons who must, by and within the law, put profits ahead of any other concern, including the welfare of society, their customers, or their own employees. Their sole concern must be productivity: the greatest possible profits against the lowest possible investment. The filmmakers' conclusion is that, if a corporation is indeed a person, it is (according to the World Health Organization diagnostic checklist) a psychopath— that is, utterly without conscience or a sense of moral responsibility. It's not surprising then, that while corporations have brought great wealth and a tremendous array of previously unavailable—or even unknown—products to the Western world, they have also spawned great ills: pollution, cancers, instruments of war, and even war itself, abuse of workers at home and abroad, the destruction of small family businesses, and much more.

It would be tempting, but completely unfair, to blame corporate leaders, many of whom are people of goodwill and moral depth, who do all they can to humanize an essentially inhuman structure. The real culprits are ourselves—those of us who buy goods made by corporations or depend on services delivered by them (that's all of us!); those of us who buy and sell stocks with the goal of collecting dividends, but with no sense or concern for what the human cost may be.

"There is no such thing as an 'ethical fund,'" a friend who is a market analyst told me awhile ago. He went on to explain that, in his view, corporate structures have so many layers that purchasing stocks in an "ethical" company would almost always be supporting a parent corporation that was involved in something dirty or destructive elsewhere. He gave a simple example: A high-profile film production company, beloved for its trademark high-quality children's and family movies is also, through other companies it owns, the world's largest single producer of pornographic films.

This corporate facet of "productivity" is concerned only with the bottom line. There is, in this particular world, one immutable moral law: "Thou shalt make money." Any thou who doesn't do so is quickly jettisoned.

In fact, it's often even worse than that.

Even in rich North America, workforces numbering in the hundreds, or sometimes the thousands, are laid off by corporations not because they are not financially profitable, but because they are just not profitable enough. The corporation, driven by its literally mindless greed for bottom-line productivity, has found some other more productive place to invest.

I've lost count of the number of highly intelligent, competent, diligent people, employed at high levels in a broad range of occupations, who have confessed their fear to me that they could lose their job at any moment. Many add that it would be in part a relief to be fired, so toxic has their work environment become to them.

A few years ago, there were two men in particular, good friends with whom I met regularly (still do): Dana and Matthias were both fifty-ish, well educated, experienced, proven, motivated, and had worked for many years with exemplary success in the financial world. Both had risen to senior management level: Matthias at the head office of a national bank and Dana at the TSX, Canada's primary stock exchange.

Although friends and colleagues considered his lack of confidence ludicrous, Matthias worried that he had risen past the level of his competence, that he was not adept enough as a manager of people, or of the ridiculous amount of stress he was under—that he was not productive enough and would soon be found out. He fretted out loud about the effect it would have on his family, the likelihood that he would lose his house if he lost his job. The situation drove him into depression.

Dana, on the other hand, had no qualms about his level of productivity. He knew he could do the job and do it well. He saw, however, serious flaws in the system that would prevent the job from being done properly. Unfortunately, there were people in the tier above him who had a vested interest in maintaining the system as it was, regardless of the flaws Dana tried, with increasing frustration, to point out. He could hear the clock ticking more loudly each day.

After a couple of years of grinding his teeth and doing the best he could in a compromised situation, Dana got the ax. He was both relieved and anxious that, now in his fifties, he would not be able to find work that was satisfying, either financially or emotionally. Matthias, on the other hand, was able to stay and flourish. Both are conscious of being on a journey that includes refusing to submit their assessment of their own selves to the prevailing paradigms of productivity. And both have found guides for their journey among the poor.

Dana, Matthias, and Susan are all people who have the tools to thrive in this "productivity environment," but all three have still found that environment to be destructive. I suspect that their experience is, in fact, the norm—that a great many of even those who ride the wave with uncommon success still harbor the fear that they will get sucked under or that what they are spending their lives on doesn't, after all, matter that much; that they do battle with a creeping sense of pointlessness.

(A friend of mine is the chair of one of Toronto's largest law firms. Every now and then I ask him, in regard to his work, if he's having any fun. He always looks at me like I have two heads.)

Mandy took a fierce pride in her own brand of productivity, but the very nature of it was destructive, and it dragged her deeper and deeper into a dark hole. At one point, I heard a rumor that she was huddled in a cheap hotel room in Vancouver's infamous East Hastings neighborhood, with a needle stuck in her arm, taking on whoever came through the door. There was another rumor a couple of years later that she had died there of AIDS. Just a few days ago, as I write this, I learned at a gathering of some of the survivors of those days that she miraculously survived it all, got out, and is somehow making a go of it as a single mom. Sadly, it was a memorial that had brought us together—a memorial for Toko, who actually had died of AIDS-related causes.

So if living for the purpose of productivity can be this damaging even to those who are able to be productive, imagine the toll it takes on those who can't. Many of the people of the Sanctuary community have been so wracked by early life trauma (abuse, abandonment, and the more adult ills that are their usual result: addictions, criminal records, homelessness, psychological problems) that they have been shoved to the outer limits of society. Others have been discarded because of chronic physical or mental illness or disability. Some once had a "normal" life (whatever that is), but the world changed and they couldn't make the adjustment. They are so far out of step with our productive society that they have ended up dwelling in a modern version of the "lake of fire" referred to by John the Revelator: the city dump, in the valley below the south "Garbage Gate" of Jerusalem, where the fires burned constantly and the figures of the societal outcasts who subsisted there could be seen from above, drifting wraithlike through the smoke, squabbling over the leavings of their betters.

This can't be the way any of us were meant to live.

Surely Jesus had something else in mind when he said, "If a man remains [dwells, lives] in me and I in him, he will bear much fruit" (John 15:5).

While a vintner would freely speak of a vine as producing grapes and of the business of the vineyard as the production of wine and would have all the concerns of any businessperson about the productivity of the whole operation, it all comes back to the foundational fact that the vine must be fruitful.

A corporation can be productive without being fruitful. It can make truckloads of money for its shareholders while doing significant harm to the environment, its employees, and society in general. A vine, on the other hand, cannot be fruitful without also being productive.

To be fruitful, it has to grow. It needs the proper amounts of rain and sun, nutrients in the soil, the careful application of fertilizers, protective coverings, pruning shears, and even, in some cases and at the proper time, frost. A vine that has been damaged needs even more intensive care. But no vintner expects even the healthiest vine to produce peaches or even a variety of grape other than what was planted. In other words, the vine has to be entirely and utterly what it was made to be in the first place. It has to be appreciated and cultivated as such and not required to be something else.

I grew up in a very high functioning, "productive" family—that is, a family with the capacity to surf the wave of societal requirement (school, church, business, etc.) with success. Although I had been involved in various kinds of outreach work in the inner city since my teens, it wasn't until I began hanging out every day with the Arthurs of this world that I began to realize my own addiction to productivity and my corresponding insistence on evaluating human beings according to their ability, or lack thereof, to be competitive in a productivity-oriented environment. People like Arthur, Dave, Sheldon, Mandy, and many others, once I began to view them as friends and companions on the journey, began by their inability to be competitive (at least in any way normally approved of by society) to reveal to me that even I had submitted my understanding of the gospel to this diabolical paradigm: I seriously thought that the work of God in an individual's life, apart from saving his or her soul, was to make that person productive.

I worked hard with some of those friends to get them to the point where they could meet the criteria of a culture that valued them only if their efforts contributed to the gross national product. Most times, my efforts were fantastically unsuccessful, at least on those terms. Because God says over and over in Scripture that people who are poor, excluded, depressed, oppressed, vulnerable, unsuccessful, inconsequential, sick, or weak are precious to him, I had to ditch my old paradigms of what makes a person valuable and look for another one—the one that Jesus teaches.

This is freeing for me, too, because I have, like Susan, wondered who I am when the gifts I have are rejected or are not sufficient for a given situation. And, like Mandy, I have been seduced by the rush of knowing that I can (sometimes) accomplish things that others can't, even if the end of it is ultimately destructive.

Those of my "poor" friends who have become productive became fruitful first. Along many a winding, backtracking, slippery path we have stumbled together, away from the illusionary goals we thought we needed to attain and toward the fulfilling, though often frustratingly slow, growth for which we are discovering our hearts actually yearn.

We thought we wanted or needed to accomplish great things. Some of us have discovered the peculiar, deadly emptiness of accomplishing much, only to realize it means little. Others have tried and failed so often that each failure only confirms the awful suspicion that we are ourselves worthless, unlovely, without hope. We are finding, though, as we prop each other up and stagger a few yards closer to home, that as we move away from *accomplishment* (what we can do) as the benchmark of our human value, we begin to understand that embracing who God created us to be (our *essence*) is the signpost we must look for on the Way.

It means much when we keep our hearts fixed on our ultimate destination. Our addictions, whether to success or crack cocaine, have a way of becoming ends in themselves, leading us off the Way into endless mazes or dead-end alleys. We forget, or never knew, where we are going. We wander aimlessly from one unsatisfying experience to another.

My friends and I call each other back to the true path when we have gotten distracted or lost. We remind each other to keep our heads up and eyes forward. We pay attention both to the path we tread—this Jesus, who is the Way—and to the glow on the horizon. For when we remember that we are going Home, that our true destination is God himself, we are no longer *wandering*, but *journeying*.

CHAPTER 10

FROM ACCOMPLISHMENT TO ESSENCE

What is man that you are mindful of him,
and the son of man that you care for him?
Yet you have made him a little lower than the heavenly
beings and crowned him with glory and honor.
—Psalm 8:4–5 ESV

On a wall of battered, honey-colored brick, beside the fireplace in Sanctuary's drop-in room, hangs a painting. This is not a gallery in the Louvre; the artist is not Rembrandt. Art aficionados might describe its style as "naive": bright yellow flowers of an unidentifiable genus leap like flames from a squat, cylindrical white vase. The vase appears to lie on a dark red circle—a platter perhaps, which in turn is perched precariously on the edge of what might be a mysteriously shaped green tabletop. The background is a field of highly textured brown and beige. There is a bold "SG" in the lower right corner.

Brush and palette knife have carved dramatic furrows in the thick paint. There is nothing tentative about the execution of this painting. It vibrates with life, hope, enthusiasm.

Steve was fifty-nine when he created this painting—his first-ever adult work of art. His "home" at the time, or at least his regular sleeping spot, was the ATM vestibule of a bank opposite city hall. He felt a little safer there than in the doorway of a shop or the stairwell of a parking garage: The surveillance camera was monitored by a security guard inside the bank. Even so, he was assaulted once by some benighted soul even more desperate than he, who must have imagined that Steve, by virtue of long proximity to vast amounts of cash, should surely have acquired some of it, perhaps by osmosis.

Like his beautiful, powerful painting, there were few hints on Steve's exterior as to his true origins. Shaggy white hair and beard, his mustache yellowed by nicotine at the corners of his mouth. Gaunt, stooped. Dark and weary eyes set deep beneath black brows. The same thick, unraveling sweater and baggy jeans week after week, month after month.

In other words, he looked like a typical older street guy when he first showed up. Somebody standing in line at a nearby meal program had told him the food was better at Sanctuary, and that was enough. It was a cold, empty feeling nevertheless, and he wasn't sure at first why he kept coming back.

Steve's downward slide had been long and lonely. Most of our people are driven to the streets by destructive families rampant with alcohol, drugs, psychosis, and the many traumas direct and indirect of physical and sexual abuse. Many have bounced from foster home to foster home, on to juvenile detention and beyond. Not Steve.

He grew up in a solid family and began working for a living straight out of high school, starting in the mailroom and later forging a career in office services. For thirty-five years he moved modestly but steadily upward, managing office equipment and internal communications.

During that time, he lived with and cared for his mother, whose mind was slowly being picked clean of memories by Alzheimer's. A couple of years after she died, the recession of the late eighties began to throttle the company he worked for; its profit margins and stock values declined steadily. At fifty-five years of age, Steve was handed a severance package, including a pension that wouldn't come due for ten more years, and shown the door.

Steve tried to find work, but the marketplace was glutted with men like him, whose age and experience would create tensions with the younger, faster, cheaper people who would be their bosses in any prospective new job. Furthermore, the rise of the Internet was changing the way companies communicated, both internally and externally, rendering much of what he had done for so many years obsolete.

His severance package kept him going for quite a while: He managed his money carefully, made no extravagant purchases, and moved from the airy high-rise apartment he had lived in for ages into a tiny bachelor pad in the basement of a house. When his severance money ran out, he discovered that he didn't qualify for welfare. He had that pension, he was told, and would have to cash it in early at a fraction of its value, exhaust that money too, then reapply.

Steve's landlord was kind and patient, but he had a family to support and a mortgage to pay. The time came when he couldn't afford to lose another month's rent. Steve sold his furniture and gave the proceeds to the landlord against his back rent. Then he filled a backpack with clothing and headed out to the streets.

Imagine this: Everything else in your life stays the same—your job, your family and friends, your social network, your home—but each night, when you open the door to your bedroom, it changes magically into the entrance vestibule of a downtown bank. The interior of the bank is brightly lit, but empty except for a night cleaner. The vestibule has two ATMs on each side wall, an abundance of fluorescent light, a security camera (which you bless), and a large rubber-backed mat, soggy with the peculiar gritty brown slip that drips from slushy boots in winter, covering the floor.

This is where you will sleep. Or try to. You roll the mat up and place it to one side, knowing that the cleaner will wake you in a couple of hours to replace it with a fresh one and mop the patch of floor where you lie. He will be polite and patient; he is Filipino and will work alone through the dark night half a world away from his wife and children. He has told you he prays for them as he works, calculating the time difference in his mind: They are just now waking up in a shack built from materials extracted from the garbage dump that surrounds it. You will be grateful then for the added comfort of the fresh mat, but for now you must take the sleeping bag from your backpack, still damp from last night, and spread it on the cold, wet terrazzo floor. The backpack is now empty but for an extra sweater and a pair of socks. You are wearing everything else you own.

The vestibule is out of the wind, but it's unheated, and the temperature outside has dropped well below freezing. You sit on the sleeping bag, remove your boots, and place them and the backpack in the corner near where your head will rest, as far as possible from the door. You've learned the hard way that any pair of boots that can be easily snatched by another homeless person will be. A brief internal debate: wear the parka you scored from a clothing bank to bed, knowing you will be hot and cramped after an hour or so, or take it off now and shiver? You have been wandering the streets for hours, waiting until after midnight to bed down because the traffic to and from the ATMs makes it pointless to arrive any earlier. You are so chilled and tired that you decide to keep it on.

So you lie there on your side, a toque pulled down over your ears and forehead, the bag zippered to your chin, listening to the hiss of the car tires rolling past, watching the cycle of green, yellow, red from the traffic lights on the corner. You are bone-weary, desperate for all the sleep you can get before six a.m., when the security guard will wake you. You'll need to rise, bundle your stuff quickly, and be gone before the first wave of customers arrives at the ATMs. The guard will be irritated if you are not, and you can't afford to irritate him. But every ligament, every muscle is tight as a guitar string. Your feet are throbbing. The numbness in your toes gives way to a painful rush of blood as they warm up. Sleep, despite your weariness, will not come quickly.

How would the rest of your life change if this was your reality every night? Would it change the way you relate to the kids in the morning, as you call them from warm, safe beds, prepare their breakfast, hustle them out the door to school? How much more difficult would it be to bear with the challenging behavior of a work colleague, prioritize your daily tasks, gather those sundry bits of information, and order them before a critical midmorning meeting? What feeling would rise within you when, already dragging, you hit that midafternoon energy lull—knowing that going to bed a little earlier tonight is not an option, that you will wake tomorrow morning wearier still than you did today? Could you enjoy supper with your family, or an evening out with friends, if the cold ache in your hip and shoulder reminded you throughout of the terrazzo "mattress" awaiting you? How hard would it be to say a gracious "good night!" to the conviviality, the safety of that circle, when you remembered the gnawing fear that last night had propped your heavy eyelids open, despite the camera and security guard? What would happen to you if this went on for a week? A month? A year?

Steve's new reality extended far beyond his sleeping arrangements. Endless days trudging across the city in search of the next free meal: crowded church basements, lineups of hungry, dirty, strung out, angry people. Snoozing for five minutes here, ten minutes there in coffee shops—propping himself up carefully and facing away from the service counter so the manager wouldn't realize he was sleeping. Searching through bins in every drop-in he attended for some kind of footwear that was watertight. Settling, finally, for several strips of duct tape to bind the soles of his own disintegrating boots. Avoiding most meaningful human connection. Isolated. There was one man he hung with for a while, but he got pinched for shoplifting, went off to jail, and Steve never saw him again.

By the time Steve found his way to Sanctuary, he had been on the streets for six months. Spending every ounce of energy on merely surviving had stripped him of almost every vestige of the normal, productive citizen he had once been. He was thin, pale, grimy, but the greatest damage had been done to his sense of identity. He had become secretive, grim; his one hope was to somehow hang on until his pension came due.

When I first met him and asked him if he had a place or was staying outside, he claimed that oh, yes, certainly he had a place. He inferred a rooming house in a vague location (he sensed that my credulity could be stretched only so far) and said that he only attended drop-ins out of a general sort of curiosity and because, his finances currently being a little stretched, the meals were a welcome change from what he could afford himself.

And when, not long after, I saw him in the wee hours of a bitter winter morning huddled in the ATM vestibule, I said nothing to him about it. He was trying to maintain some shred of dignity; he wasn't yet sure that I, or other people at Sanctuary, could be trusted. We asked him periodically if he was content in his mythical room. Months passed before he could admit what he suspected we already knew—that he was homeless and destitute.

Although Steve was one of hundreds in our community in the same situation, he was filled with shame. He was convinced that he had been so thoroughly discarded by society because he had nothing left of any value to offer it. Nothing he had accomplished in the past had any meaning now. He had the sense that he was not truly welcome anywhere, that the best he could hope for was to be tolerated, granted a minimal, grudging, faceless charity.

The first clue he had that he might actually belong was, ironically, an event sponsored by World Vision, an international relief and development organization, called "Thirty Hour Famine." It was a kind of starve-a-thon—wealthy Western participants, mostly church youth groups, gathered pledges and went thirty hours without food while playing games and camping out in church buildings as a way of raising money for and expressing solidarity with famine-stricken people in other nations. Steve "starved" along with a group at Sanctuary made up primarily of teenagers, mostly because he'd get to spend thirty hours straight in a warm, dry building. He discovered that a hunger more voracious than the one sated by the massive breakfast at the end of the event had been addressed. He had enjoyed immensely being with all those young people who had treated him with affection and respect and who had listened intently as he described the poverty on the streets of their own city. To his surprise, he had gone in one night from nonentity to "expert."

Steve had spent a few years becoming progressively more isolated, wary of any real human connection, but he now began to slowly reverse that process, seeking opportunities to check out other aspects of the community. He attended Friday afternoon art-and-games drop-ins mostly because they didn't draw the huge crowd of hungry, strung out street people that came on Wednesdays and Thursdays for a meal. He only intended to quietly hang out, observe things from the perimeter, but when Sharon Tiessen (Sanctuary's resident artist) stuck a paintbrush in his hand and stood him in front of a blank canvas, everything changed.

Sometimes when I'm trying to describe Steve's first painting to people, I'll say, "You know that famous Van Gogh painting of sunflowers? It's like Van Gogh painted another version of that just after he dropped some acid ..." Everybody who saw the painting loved it immediately—it just vibrates with energy. For a while, I introduced him to visitors as "Vincent Van Steve." I think Steve was as flummoxed by what he had produced as anybody. But the change in him was unmistakable: Old Steve, the poor, beaten-down street guy, became Steve Grant, the Artist.

Steve has been, and continues to be, on a remarkable journey. Becoming an artist himself was the first step toward the Artist who had created him. There are a lot of people around besides Sharon who have had a part in calling out of Steve the true essence of who he is—and he, of course, has been pouring that essence back into their lives as well. Discovering that "successful" people recognize that he has much to offer them as an artist, or as a teacher of street wisdom, has been an incredibly dignifying experience. Being valued as a friend and brother by people like Matthias and Dana is helping him understand that it's who he is that matters, not what he can accomplish. Steve is probably our most active and committed street outreach volunteer. Reaching out to others from a place of empathy has lit a fire in his heart.

"I can't stop caring about them," he told me recently. "It's like when my mother was dying—I couldn't just walk away from her either. I think that was preparing me for this."

It's not always a straightforward journey. Twice, we've helped him find housing, and twice, he's lost it. Once, his rooming house became unsafe because of crack addicts. Another time, there was an infestation of bedbugs (an epidemic in the city at the time). Both times, the old street mentality kicked in, and he simply returned to the streets without mentioning his problems to his friends, feeling that he had no right to complain or that nothing he said would be heard anyway. Both times, those of us who knew him well began to recognize the signs that he was back on the street before he could bring himself to admit what had happened.

That first experience of speaking to youth about street life was so powerful that Steve has volunteered for just about every opportunity to do so ever since. I remember a Q & A session he did with a youth group from a conservative evangelical church.

"Are you a born-again Christian?" someone asked him. Steve's brow furrowed; his response was hesitant.

"Well, you know, I was raised Anglican, and I've tried to live by all that …"

Steve was, I think, more than a little uncertain about all the God stuff at that point. His childhood religious experience had been cultural and nominal. Maybe he wondered where God had gone when he lost his job, a place to live, his own sense of self.

Now he's unconcerned about being Anglican[1] or anything much else—he knows who Jesus is and what he has done for him. I won't forget the sight of Steve lying back in the arms of Steve Martin, a Sanctuary staff member, and his partner and mentor in street outreach, as he was lowered beneath baptismal water. Nor will I forget the way his face beamed as he rose from the water, and the people gathered round sang "Oh, Happy Day!" Every Sunday now, I listen for Steve's fervent "Amen!" at the conclusion of our celebration of the Lord's Supper.

Now he lives with two young families who have generously welcomed him into intentional Christian community. It was a stretch at first, for a guy who had been so alone for so long. But those families have become his family, and he finally has a home.

A few years ago, when he had started to believe in the possibility of a new life but had not yet figured out how to live it, Steve concocted a plan: When his pension came due, he would buy a good backpack, a sleeping bag, and a ticket to New Zealand. He would hike alone, living out in the open, but with enough money to buy food or new shoes whenever he was in need. I feared that it was a form of slightly more dignified homelessness, an escape from the painful reality in which he still saw himself as a man with no home, a retreat back into the isolation and emptiness that had claimed him for so long.

As the time drew nearer, others close to him began quietly to voice the same kind of concerns that I had. Steve came to me and asked me what I thought—should he stay, or should he go? I told him that having a vision for your future is an important and powerful thing, that, as he had nurtured this one for so long, it should not be easily put aside. But, I confessed, I was worried that my good friend would find himself alone and friendless again, that I—we!—would miss him, that I couldn't imagine that he would quickly become as precious to others as he was to us. He must listen for God's voice in the matter.

A couple of weeks later he sidled up to me during a drop-in.

"Hey," he said with a delighted grin. "I'm not going. Oh, I'll probably go for a little visit, but I won't stay. All those young people who need to learn about poverty, all the guys still out there on the streets … this is my home. My work isn't done here yet. I have a lot more to do!"

$ $ $

Steve had, for many years, been a normal, middle-class guy—the backbone-of-society type with the accomplishments to match. But when those accomplishments ceased having an immediate value to others, it almost destroyed him, because they had defined him, not only to society, but also to himself. Losing his history of accomplishment meant he lost much of his identity. The whole range of new accomplishments that characterize his life now—artist, teacher, outreach worker, disciple, pastor, family guy—are merely expressions of the essence of who he truly is. The farther he hikes along this path, the more that true identity is revealed.

Steve wouldn't have found this path on his own, nor could he have traveled far without companionship. In fact, he specifically needed "wealthy" people as guides on the journey—people like Susan, Matthias, Dana, the Johnson-Hatlem and ElzingaCheng families he lives with now, Steve Martin and other Sanctuary staffers, Kate Jones, Dan and Anne Robins (members of our worshipping community), all those university students and youth groups, and a great many others. Through those people, who are "accomplishing" many things that society values, God has been able to speak words of healing into Steve's life. They could affirm in a way that other street people couldn't that Steve was and is inherently precious, valuable simply because he was made in God's image. Hearing this from them set him free to find a new life in Christ and to uncover gifts he had never before recognized he possessed.

The sweet little miracle in all this is that, along the way, Steve has been helping others homeward too. Witnessing his new, vibrant, "resurrected" life clambering out of the grave of the old has granted some "successful" people the much-needed hope that their own lives are also more important than the mere sum of their accomplishments. Helping Steve on his journey has reminded others that the truest "bottom line" of their own life enterprise is not the best possible differential between energy in and product out, but the fruit that is borne by a branch well rooted in and fed by the vine.

$ $ $

Steve has been one of several "guides" for Matthias. Matthias speaks frequently about his surprising first visit to Sanctuary a number of years ago—about the same time that Steve showed up, although they didn't get to know each other for quite a while.

Matthias had been invited to visit a lunchtime drop-in after a work colleague made an initial introduction. He walked the couple of blocks from the bank offices and entered a different world. Matthias, dressed in business attire, stood out in our crowd of street hustlers, panhandlers, cross-dressers, and barely-getting-by rooming house denizens. But he was welcomed cheerfully, and no one made him feel out of place.

Matthias had come expecting to "serve the homeless," but he wasn't allowed to help prepare, serve, or clean up after the meal. When he was instead invited to take a seat at a table, he at first demurred, as visitors often do. He didn't want to take a meal that someone else needed more than he did.

"Oh, just sit and eat," he was told. "You need this at least as much as anyone else here."

So, although he didn't quite understand yet what that meant, he sat and ate. And came back. And discovered he enjoyed it. Nobody cared where he worked, what he could do, or how busy or important he was. Or wasn't. At the bank, he knew he would be welcome only as long as he was productive. Here, he was welcome simply because he chose to walk through the door. It was a world away from the environment he felt was slowly sucking the life out of him.

It was a world away from his church life, too. He was in the process of leaving the church he and his family had attended for years and at which he had for some time been an elder. The church was undergoing a significant shift in direction, one that he objected to on the basis of deeply held principle. He thought God was leading him to help make the church more welcoming to people who are poor or excluded. He spoke up; he engaged in dialogue with other leaders and congregational members. Where once he had been a core leader, seeking to bring healing to a divided church, he was now being told by the leadership that he was no longer welcome to lead anything and that a "separate" ministry to the poor was not in line with the direction that the church was taking. Finally, because he had no interest in being a divisive presence and could see that others were not responding to his view, he chose to leave.

He says now that he was left adrift, felt abandoned by God, and in the process discovered how much his previous relationship with him had depended on his own strengths and efforts. He would find himself in the middle of the night, sitting on the bottom step of the stairs to his basement so as not to alarm his family as they slept two floors above, weeping at the weight of abandonment threatening to crush his soul.

There was no journey "back" to health for him, only a tough upward climb on a new, narrow, difficult track that required him to lay aside the weights he had acquired unawares and plod homeward. Good therapeutic counsel has helped guide him. So has a formal process of spiritual direction. But many of his companions on the Way—the ones who are, at times, pioneering the trail just a few steps ahead of him and, at others, needing his help to navigate a difficult bend in the track—are people like Steve, who, in the eyes of the world, have nothing.

Through Steve and other friends in the community, Matthias has learned a few things that help him live well despite the demands that remain so high in his professional life. His mere presence in our worshipping community, whether or not he says or does anything, has a significant impact. Rather than striving to be an influencer, he simply has to be who he is. This is certainly not because Sanctuary is in any way a superior form of church—on the contrary, it is small, poorly organized, highly improvisational, and unpredictable. Many of the people who lead us in prayer or worship lead lives that are impossibly messy and broken. But that's the point: God is so obviously speaking in and through them that it means that a man like Matthias no longer needs to define himself through his competence, education, or intelligence. He too is just a child of God.

People like Steve, who have so little in material terms and have for long periods had even less, have a hard-won ability to teach, in the profoundest way, the lesson of the "widow's mite." Through them, Matthias hears Jesus saying to him, "Give me all that you have, and I will give you all that you need." No longer a trite Christian aphorism, this word to Matthias means he can rest in trusting that God, not he himself, is Master of his future. It is, he says, a matter of *actually* trusting God moment by moment—not just *believing* in trusting.

A little while ago, Matthias gathered at Sanctuary with a small group that was preparing to do street outreach on a Friday night. The group was led by Steve and Doug Johnson, the Sanctuary staff member with whom Steve lives. Because there were a couple of new participants, they went around the small circle, introducing themselves.

"My name is Matthias, and I'm a member of Sanctuary's board of directors," Matthias announced when his turn came. Instantly, he wished the words back—they represented, he felt, a relapse into an old and unhealthy paradigm where accomplishment and position were of primary importance. When he told me this and I asked him what he felt he should have said, Matthias smiled his slow smile.

"My name is Matthias—and I'm a friend of Steve."

CHAPTER 11

FROM WANDERING TO JOURNEYING

They were not able to enter, because of their unbelief. Therefore,
since the promise of entering his rest still stands, let us be
careful that none of you be found to have fallen short of it.
—Author unknown, Hebrews 3:19—4:1

In my Father's house are many rooms; if it were not so, I
would have told you. I am going there to prepare a place for
you.... You know the way to the place where I am going.
—Jesus, gospel of John 14:2, 4

The hardest of the hard men on the streets are rarely the brawny, snarling types you might expect. Of middle height, if that, and usually on
the lean side, Max is on the surface a happy, chatty guy who takes
a childlike delight in dollar store gizmos and bicycles. Maybe that's
because he didn't have much of a childhood. If you knew that his father
had thrown him through a plate glass window at age eleven because
young Max had been caught stealing the old man's dope, you would
just be scratching the surface.

Max was in his early thirties when I first met him, and he had already done or was doing all the usual street survival routines: he'd been a prostitute as a youngster, had girlfriends who were also prostitutes, sold drugs, ingested copious amounts of them himself, shoplifted, panhandled, committed break and entries, fenced stolen goods, skipped bail, resisted arrest, and had done pretty much every petty or violent crime in the book, short of murder and armed robbery.

He was living down in the Rosedale Valley with his girlfriend at the time, in a lean-to made of cardboard, tree branches, green garbage bags, and scraps of plastic sheeting he'd scrounged off a construction site. He'd had a sudden, inexplicable urge to do something "normal"— maybe buy a dime of weed and go see a movie—instead of doing the usual night's hustle.

He and his girlfriend were headed for the Uptown near Bloor and Yonge when some cracker on the street told them, "Hey, they're having some kind of a do over there." Didn't even know where "over there" was, but his girlfriend had been coming to Sanctuary for years, and they wandered in. He told me later he sensed something different right from the start, and looking back, he thought he felt like he'd finally come home.

For years, he'd been the king of Allan Gardens, the guy who could be counted on to provide any amount of the best-quality crack cocaine, no wax, anytime day or night. He had this one bench he'd work from, and people who knew him would get off it immediately if they saw him step foot in the park. He remembered times he robbed other dealers because he was so wired he wanted someone to kill him. They wouldn't kill him, of course—he was making them all too much money.

In some ways, like providing the best stuff and returning top profits, he had been pretty reliable. And he had just enough of that

Charlie Manson look and action to keep everybody careful. He'd never forget the time he went off on a guy who had run out on him in a tough situation, because every morning he could still feel the long shaft of scar tissue extending into his abdomen from just below his ribs.

For a few years, after crawling out of the valley, he made steady progress. Got a place. Got a job. Stayed, mostly, away from drugs and alcohol. Drove people crazy with his constant talk about this Jesus he had found.

Once I saw a local loudmouth try to goad him into fighting, taunting him with threats and insults in front of a group of his street peers hanging around outside of Sanctuary.

"What's with Thomas?" I heard somebody say. "Beakin' off at Max like that? Has he lost his mind?"

"He'll lose his *life* if he keeps pressing Max," somebody else responded.

Max eventually walked Thomas across the street, on the pretext of taking their beef off the Sanctuary property. As it transpired, he was giving Thomas the opportunity to back down without losing face. Max merely spoke quietly to him for a minute or so. Nobody knows what he said, but Thomas's face went briefly pale, and by the time they recrossed the street, they were the best of friends.

Word spread that Max had backed down from a fight. Another bully, mistaking Max's new meekness for weakness, wouldn't take no for an answer. He pushed and goaded and pushed some more—and woke up in the hospital. Max tortured himself about it for weeks. He was trying to leave street life behind, but it kept hunting him down.

Max was, during this time, a great teacher and guide for me. He worked incredibly hard to make the tiniest of gains in his battle to escape a lifetime of abuse. I admired the visceral, minute-by-minute grittiness of his faith. When I told him that, he looked at me solemnly and declared, "Greg, if I don't give each day to God before I get out of bed in the morning, I'll die."

He meant it absolutely literally. He knew in his gut what I knew only in my head—that without complete dependence on God, there is no healing, no meaning, no true safety.

Max continued to struggle, of course. It was as if there was some final hump he could never quite get over. He would do well for a while, then feel himself starting to slip. He'd start smoking a little weed again, to take the edge off, but the panic would keep rising. He said it was like a beast within him, wild and dark, that demanded to be fed. He'd snap, finally, go on a bender, and do things that were increasingly destructive to himself and the relationships he had come to value most.

When it was over—when he was broke, sick, and exhausted— he would come back, begging forgiveness, weeping with frustration and desire for the freedom that continued to elude him. We prayed together—a whole network of people who had come to care deeply about him—studied Scripture, built more supports around him … and he'd go through the whole nasty cycle again.

It was during such a period that Matthias and Maureen came to worship with us for the first time. They had brought with them their young daughter Kayla and Kayla's friend Jaye. Matthias, since he had begun regularly joining our community for lunch on Wednesday afternoons, would, I knew, have some idea of what he might encounter. I remember wondering briefly, as we got started that Sunday night, what Maureen and the kids would make of it.

Although the "service" might have been a little rowdier than what they were used to—louder music, less decorum, more laughter, and people wandering back and forth—it was reasonably tame at first. It was when the music stopped and we began to focus our attention on the bread and wine that it got a little wild.

The physical format of our worship times is unusual. Instead of rows of chairs or pews facing a pulpit or altar, there is a large circle a few rows deep, with an open end near the platform. There is no pulpit at all. A rough old cross with cockeyed arms stands on the wooden floor in the middle of that open end; sometimes Ken circumnavigates it in his wheelchair. The band is at the back of the room, farthest away from the cross and behind all the chairs: We want to make the point physically that the band is merely part of the congregation and not the proper focus of attention. There is a row of chairs, some of them stacked, with their backs to each side wall. And in the middle of the circle is a little wooden table with wobbly legs, upon which Dan the guitar player has carved the words "In Remembrance of Me."

Max had slipped in late and had taken one of those seats with their backs to the wall just behind and slightly to one side of Matthias and Maureen. I didn't even know he was there until he began to pray out loud.

There are several people in our community who regularly pray with a directness and transparency that can be disarming or unnerving or both. And through the years, we've heard the gut-wrenching cry of many a desperate soul. But we've rarely heard the sheer, raw anguish of Max's prayer that evening.

He was racing—I could tell that from the first sentence. Max is hyperactive, among other things; when he's stressed out or strung out, his mind goes a mile a minute, and his mouth struggles to keep up.

Trying to follow him as he prayed that night was like being on a spiritual rabbit hunt: His thoughts, expressed with increasing volume and a tearing edge of grief to his voice, zigged and zagged, then disappeared down one hole and popped up again somewhere else entirely a second later.

He spoke with a searing honesty of his failures, his essential brokenness, his self-hatred. He described how ugly he seemed to himself, how nearly unbelievable it was that God could see him as anything but a squalid, ugly little monster—and how desperately he wanted to believe that he really was forgiven, redeemed, made blameless in the eyes of God. He pleaded for miracles—he called it magic, "that spark"—something, anything, that would heal him of his addiction, his memories that would attack him like a dark clawing beast that was shredding his soul.

His voice, wild and grating, soared into the vaulted ceiling, bounced around, and came back down to the rest of us like a word from on high. We were with him; we heard echoes of our own struggles and sorrows in his; we said, "Yes!" fervently in our hearts to his pleas for healing—"yes" to healing for Max,, and "yes" to healing for our own tattered souls.

At the height of his passion, Max's voice broke. There was a moment of dead silence, then he put his head back and howled a single word. A short, vulgar word. One entirely inappropriate to the decorum of a church gathering or to the sanctity of worship.[1]

I had two immediate reactions. One was the simple response, which I sensed all of our regular people shared, of saying a heartfelt "Amen." The terminology didn't matter. His language was the language of our secret hearts. Max was speaking for all of us; he was, in this moment, truly our priest.

The other and distinctly fainter reaction was to wonder how Matthias, Maureen, and the kids were doing with all this. Because Max was sitting behind them, and in the same line of sight from where I sat, and because I was watching him as he prayed—watching the tears course down his cheeks, the swinging jaw, the hands clutching his head—I happened also to see them at the moment he dropped the bomb.

There was no visible reaction from Matthias and Maureen. Their heads were respectfully bowed, their eyes closed, faces composed. Church faces. But the children's heads came up with a jerk; their eyes went big, then narrowed. They took a cautious peek over their shoulders at the excitable gent behind them, and I knew what must be going on in their minds.

"Did he really just say what I think he said? Here? In a church? Hmm. No, can't be. Nobody's freaking out …"

I wondered vaguely if I ought to connect with the four of them when we took our usual break a bit later—help them process what had just happened. I was a little concerned that they would just find it all terribly inappropriate and offensive and not come back. On the other hand, my ungracious self thought, *It's not my job to make things easy for tourists from the suburbs.* And I forgot about it.

But Matthias and Maureen kept coming back. On the surface it was an unlikely fit. Matthias you've met already. Maureen is a public school French teacher of sunny disposition. They and their four (truly!) lovely children are firmly ensconced in upper-middle-class Outer Suburbia, doing many of the things that typical Outer Suburbanites do. They're wealthy, apparently secure and comfortable, lead balanced, ordered, healthy lives, and have no discernable "edge." Matthias works nearby and has for a number of years served as a member of Sanctuary's board of directors; there is perhaps some rationale for him seeking a deeper connection. But there really is no obvious reason why Maureen would choose, as she has so clearly done in the ensuing years, to find a spiritual home among such a derelict fragment of society.

I asked her recently if she remembered that first time she had come with Matthias, Kayla, and Jaye to worship with us. Yes, she said, she remembered it very clearly.

"Do you remember Max's prayer? What he said in the middle of it?"

"Uh-huh," she said. "I certainly do."

This was a very contained response for Maureen, who generally gives the impression of having a truly hilarious joke lodged within her, bubbling up and threatening to burst out at any second.

"I always wondered what you made of it …"

Maureen looked at me with her dancing blue eyes and spoke with an uncharacteristic gravity: "That was the moment I knew this would be a safe place for me."

She continued on to speak of her deep hunger for "unmitigated reality"—the possibility of being thoroughly honest about her own internal needs and battles and of receiving the gift of such honesty from others. She longed to break bread and drink wine, she said, for true communion, the knowledge that "we"—some undefined group of pilgrims—were walking the same road in unity with each other, a unity found in and leading to Christ himself. Her middle-class (that is, wealthy) church and life experience, where every messy thing is so carefully contained, every surface so diligently polished, had left her with a sense of discontentment, of empty wandering. She wanted to get her hands on Jesus.

(She also mentioned that Max had approached her and the children later and apologized for his language.)

Max's prayer was both priestly and prophetic. Here, he seemed to say, is a band of poor, withered souls who have no option but to turn from the substitutes with which we have numbed our pain, our consciences, and face the Christ. You may, if you choose, walk along with us. We have not even the strength to pretend that we are okay. Because we do not have the resources to rent, buy, or build comfortable stopping places along the path, we cannot afford to turn aside but must set our sights on the distant glow on the horizon—the lights of the City across the river, the Last House, the Home of the Father. The mere gleam of it reminds us of where we are headed, even when the path ahead momentarily disappears from view. If we keep our faces turned toward it, it shines brightest even as darkness falls. We can for a time not even move forward, but this spot where we huddle is imbued with a flicker of that place's glory. It's enough to warm us, give us a little courage, and grant us the hope that when night next drops we will be a day's journey closer home.

The quote from Hebrews 3:19—4:1 at the head of this chapter refers to the people of Israel, whom God had liberated from slavery. After a relatively short, dramatic journey from Egypt (somewhere between a few months' and a few years' duration, depending on how you read the text), the people stood on the borders of the Promised Land—the land of rest, a place of their own, after four hundred years of backbreaking, soul-crushing slavery. Twelve men spied out the land; all agreed it was a good, fruitful place, but ten declared that the people there were strong—giants!—and the cities well fortified. "We seemed like grasshoppers in our own eyes," they said, and the entire herd, perhaps a million people, turned around and scuttled back out into the desert (Num. 13:33).

There they wandered back and forth for forty years, until, but for Joshua and Caleb, the two more optimistic spies, all those who had been twenty years of age or older at the time of turning back had perished. Forty years of living out the mean, parched view of themselves as a rabble of ex-slaves, with no identity, no hope, no home. So entrenched was this self-perception that they could not conceive of themselves the way God did: a nation, a mighty people under God, pioneers, builders, and defenders of a land in which every tribe had a province, every family a pasture or farm, every person a home. Without a destination ahead of them, the best they could imagine was going back to Egypt, back to slavery. They didn't even make it there: Forty years they wandered, a great, complaining, fractious, directionless mob, until one by one, their bodies dropped in the dust.

Max, my dear, dear friend and brother, seems also to come to the very borders of the land, gaze longingly at its goodness, drink a little from the rivers there, and conclude that it is not for a slave such as him. He fears the giants (they seem so much larger than the ones I face), cannot imagine that they might be slain. He turns and heads back out into the wilderness for a while longer.

I still see him from time to time. He keeps getting thinner. He seems aimless, lost.

"Can't stop right now," he'll say—or, too often, it's I who have to say it. We'll make a date to get together, but he doesn't usually show. He still comes to worship with us sometimes. He never lasts for the entire thing.

Still, he continues in some fashion to be a guide or at least a companion on the journey and not only to me or Maureen. As I was writing this story, I received an e-mail from Mel, another member of our community. Although Mel comes from a place of privilege, as I do, and is an incredibly talented artist, dancer, and poet, she has many deep struggles that require her also to keep her eyes on the horizon and to lean heavily on her companions on the way when she can't.

"We're just pretty fragile, aren't we?" she wrote. "I ran into Max on my way home from work and we talked briefly. Then I took the street-car and a woman stood in front of me, jonesing … I'm sure people were staring at her, but I didn't want to stare at her too. Her body was acting out this incredible desperation. It's so weird being in the city, like God is speaking all the time, but most of us are deaf. And I keep seeing people who reflect who I am …

"I had a semi-productive day at work. But when no one was around, I put my head down on the desk in the crook of my arm, and just sat like that as a wave swept over me.

"Somehow Jesus finds us in this foggy cold dirty city? Yes, I guess … 'we hope for what we do not yet have.'[2] I feel so strange and quiet and sad, waiting for the nearness of the Lamb."

In another e-mail, Mel mentioned Max again—he had come to worship on a Sunday—as well as a young woman she had visited in the hospital, who had just given birth while living on the streets, and two more homeless women "who blessed me with their hugs. But," she continued, giving expression to the reality that this journeying together is no easy matter, "something about those two women just gets to me, and I always feel like crying after I talk with them …"

For Maureen, Max in some strange, deep fashion announced that she had found one of those places that bear some traces of the true home she seeks—perhaps in the way that the writer of Hebrews said that the material sanctuary in which the worshippers of his day found refuge was a "copy and shadow" of the true one in heaven (Heb. 8:5).

Max, for a several years at least, found in his fellow journeyers the support he needed to walk away from destruction and toward health and home. Although he appears to be "wandering" now, "there remains … a Sabbath rest for the people of God" (Heb. 4:9–10). I hope still that he will "rest from his own work" and thus find it.

For Mel and me, our companionship with Max graphically reminds us of the lie inherent in the idea that "the destination matters not—the journey's the thing!" A journey with no destination is mere wandering. And as Mel has written in yet another e-mail message, "One thing for sure, the wandering is not really wandering … but waging war, running, hiding, attacking, defending, fighting for your life. Fighting to feel something, to internalize that I mean something, that I matter, that everything/anything matters …"

There is no healing to be found in such a battle. Only deeper and deeper weariness, wounds and bruises and weeping sores. We have seen both sides of it in Max—the clarity of the journey, as painful and impossible as it may seem at times, and the consuming, confusing hollowness of wandering, although it may appear in the moment to be the easier, more comfortable route. We recognize it also in ourselves.

Mel continues to feel at times that she really is just lost in the desert. Despite her intelligence, courage, and beauty, despite a faith that is much deeper than she herself is able to recognize, Jesus often seems very far away.

"Land of rest," she says. "Freedom, shalom, milk and honey … I want very much to know what all this is, but it feels like the other powers are stronger in the here and now."

Who can read that and not relate to it? And yet, because of companions like Max and Mo and the homeless women who hug her, Mel was also able to write this: "The people I meet at Sanctuary and on the street help me to find the Way … because Jesus reveals himself to me through them. I'm learning to see Jesus in a new way. Before, I experienced God in this way: I got a sense of his bigness, his majesty, his awesome presence. But he was entirely God; he was most definitely not like me. Nowadays, if I experience a sense of the divine at all, it is quite different. Now, I have stumbled across the still-bleeding savior, lying limply at the base of the cross where they have taken him down. And he has been pierced and beaten, one eye is swollen shut and purply-black, his feet are oozing, his nose is broken … It hurts to look at this Jesus. I think: if he survives this, he'll have scars all over …

"This is the Jesus I meet in our community. I encounter the Suffering One, the Afflicted One. The Man of Sorrows. I hear stories of pain and hurt, and only afterward do I realize (and sometimes I don't realize it) that I've been on holy ground.

"I also see these very same people dance and laugh, give each other tips on detox centers … sometimes I might share an ice cream with one of them, or a hot drink, and some time spent in a coffee shop. Sometimes I might share the bread and the wine with a few of them. And this too is holy ground. Jesus reveals himself here to me: glimpses he gives of a true and worthy kingdom."

And this, to a group of her fellow journeyers: "This morning I sat in a chair in the sunlight and put on a few CDs to listen to some songs: 'When I Survey the Wondrous Cross' … How long, how long O Lord, will you forget me? Yet I will trust in your unfailing love … 'It Is Well with My Soul' … and so on.

"I prayed short but honest prayers, about how I felt every good thing in me is tainted, and how my compassion and care for people is so shallow, and how I don't understand Jesus or even really know him. But I do trust that having put that out there, God will honor my prayers by teaching me more about himself. And I guess he does that by being with me. So that's something to look forward to.

"I prayed for you, and I felt very lucky that we walk a common road, that I have all you wonderful people as company.

"It seems sometimes that God gives us such simple (by simple, I mean pure) and beautiful things—friends who really care, and a spot of sunlight.

"love you,

mel."

$ $ $

Because Mel, Max, Mo, Matthias, Chris, Steve, and a host of others are there to lead me on or push me from behind, I too find the courage to walk another day's journey.

"Keeping my eyes on the destination," "keeping my feet on the path," "entering the land of rest": these are different ways of expressing my need to stay rooted in the one true Vine. When I look away—when I wander or turn back into the desert—I have chosen to seek sustenance elsewhere. I succumb, then, to the temptation to "forge my own destiny," "define myself by my own experience," and any number of other bold, ultimately deadly phrases. The truth is that I am probably seeking an easier, more comfortable path and in doing so, am walking away from the very person God has created me to be—and from God himself.

My friends who, like Max, have so little to fall back on give a quick and potent confirmation to Max's assertion that "if I don't give every day to God, I'll die." The wheels fall off very quickly in their lives. But I have so many resources—I am so wealthy—that it's possible to maintain the fiction that I am doing just fine, thanks. I can continue to be productive and may even be able to spin things enough that I look fruitful, too.

Through the years, I have buried dozens of my friends, victims of long-term substance abuse, overdose, illnesses contracted through dirty needles or insanely risky sexual practices, suicide, murder, terminal sexual assaults, and the kind of absurd accidents that can only befall people who have spent years being mostly high or drunk and chronically tired, hungry, and afraid. But Max's words are as true for me as for them. The death I die may be a slower, quieter thing, a withering rather than an explosion, but it's just as lethal. The Maxes of this world remind me, both in the positive and in the negative, of the truth of this.

I want to live, truly live. I want to grow, to know the sustaining sap of the vine rushing through me, and to bring forth a fantastic abundance of fruit. I want my companions on the journey to be able to share that fruit, as I share theirs. Some day, when the journey's done and we've finally arrived home, all us little branches will hoist a glass with the Vintner himself and with the Vine too. It'll be a well-aged, thoroughly intoxicating vintage—when held up to the light, a rich, deep, deep red.

FROM SUFFERING TO GLORY

I consider that our present sufferings are not worth comparing with the glory that will be revealed in us.
—Paul, Romans 8:18

In bringing many sons to glory, it was fitting that God ... should make the author of their salvation perfect through suffering.
—Author unknown, Hebrews 2:10

COLM

My name is Colm, and I'm an alcoholic.

He rolls the wheel on the Zippo and lights another spliff.

Hi, Colm!

Stretched out on the bed with an ashtray on his bare stomach, he inhales deeply and holds it as long as he can. They call it the "marijuana maintenance program" in the twelve-step rooms, with a sardonic lift of the eyebrow and an understanding smile that always gets him a little riled. Well, they can recite their self-righteous little mantras all they want—it's medicine as far as Colm is concerned. He's been sober fifteen years now, and weed is a big part of the reason why.

He hears the sudden *shhhh* of the shower and, over top of it, Mario humming jauntily. Nice guy, Mario. Almost pretty, but not stuck up about it. Still, now that it's over with, Colm is glad to have the darkened room to himself for a few minutes. Getting a little more mellow with every toke.

A nice little crib he has, too. Nothing special about the building itself, just an aging rectangular apartment tower, but some good furniture in the living room, tastefully decorated, very clean, almost austere. A great southwest view from the balcony, overlooking the Village and toward the towers of the downtown core. The bedroom is a little larger than you'd expect. Colm reclines upon the plush king-size bed, only his feet tucked beneath the tossed-back white duvet.

Maybe Mario will let him stay a few days. He cooks, too, makes his own pasta …

Colm is starting to doze when the bedroom door, which has been just barely ajar, bangs open, making a cracking sound as the handle hits the wall. There is a lean, dark figure in the doorway, backlit by the hall light, swearing.

Colm lurches upright, shrieking.

A foul, bitter hand sweeps aside the gentling clouds of the dope, reaches under his rib cage, and thrusts inward, upward until it clamps on his esophagus. It squeezes until his eyes feel like they will pop from their sockets. He can hardly see through the maroon haze clouding his vision, but he can hear the dark form thumping deliberately across the floor toward him.

"Stop yer caterwaulin', ye manky little git," it grates at him, absurdly retaining that musical Irish lilt despite its slurring rage. "C'mere. I'll give ye somethin' to squall about. How can a boy of mine be such a puling little fairy, anyways?"

Colm is caught by an ankle, dragged to the foot of the bed, spun around, and slapped several times across the face. Next, he is held by the neck while his shoulders and chest are pummeled with a fist like a rock—he always works top to bottom. Colm is crying now, trying desperately to stop because the voice is hollering at him that it will beat him senseless if he doesn't quiet down. But he can't; his arms are still so bruised and sore from the last time. Finally, a punch in the stomach knocks the air out of him. For a long moment, unable to draw a breath, he thinks—hopes—that he is dying. But he knows it isn't over yet.

Those iron hands flip him over. One, planted in the middle of his back, presses him to the mattress while the other yanks the pajama bottoms off him, careful even in this malicious fit not to tear them.

Foul breath, and that grinding voice close to his ear. The unholy liturgy he has heard for as long as he can remember:

"And this, ye poncy little maggot. This is for yer wickedness. This is what you deserve, and all yer good for."

So much pain. Inside and out. An army of pain invading him, establishing a beachhead, sending out sorties to claim new territory. Colm abandons the defenses; he capitulates. He dies. Blackness …

A voice, another voice, gentle and worried, calls his name. He opens his eyes—no, his eyes were already open; the darkness clears. Mario. Sitting beside him on the bed, a towel still draped around his neck. His dark, liquid eyes wide with fear and concern.

"Colm. Colm. Are you back? Wow. Oh, good. Phew. You know it's me, Mario, right? Okay, sorry, I don't mean to be condescending, but you were really kinda gone there for a bit. I tripped when I was coming back into the bedroom, banged into the door with my knee—ow, it still kinda hurts—and you just, uh, just lost it. You scared me."

Colm looks at him, still not able to speak. His back and neck are killing him. Mario strokes his forehead and cheek, the little silver pendant cross around his neck swinging free as he leans forward.

"Are you going to be okay? I came in to tell you I have to go in to work for the afternoon. You can stay here if you want, though. Why don't you? Seriously, are you okay? Yeah?"

Colm nods finally, clears his throat, mumbles a thank-you. They are silent and motionless for a time, Colm spread out rigid on the bed, Mario perched hesitantly beside him. Growing awkwardness. Eventually Mario reaches out a slender finger and runs it over the bumps on Colm's forearm and wrist. Colm can see him carefully framing the question.

"What are these from?"

Mario hadn't noticed them last night at the club or in the darkened bedroom in the wee hours of this morning. Now he's wondering if it's a manifestation of That Which Shall Not Be Named in a Bedroom.

"They're lesions!" Colm barks, unintentionally. His voice is still recovering from the grip of that awful, throttling hand. Mario is understandably taken aback. Neither Colm's tone nor the word "lesions" has done anything to allay his fears.

"Calcium deposits. From … injuries I received as a child," Colm says more gently. He reaches out and pats Mario's knee. *Thank you, thank you for your tenderness. Thanks for not being put off. I'm harmless.*

Mario's clouded face clears. He bounces to his feet and across the room to that exquisite dresser, speaking over his shoulder as he fishes around for underwear and socks.

"I'll be home around five. I can make us a nice rigatoni, some salad, a little cabernet—oh, I forgot you don't drink." Turning to grin at him. "Never mind. I can certainly bring home a little more 'Tina.'"

When Mario has gone, Colm pours a glass of orange juice, takes it out to the balcony, and lights up a smoke from a pack he found on the coffee table. His racing heart began to slow down immediately after the door closed behind Mario. *A very trusting guy,* he thinks. *Considering he really has no idea who I am and has apparently figured out that I have no place else to go.* Not so trusting himself, Colm wonders what the game is. Whatever. He's here at least until this evening.

After a time, his legs begin to ache. He tries sitting down on a plastic chair on the balcony, hoping to enjoy a little more of a pleasant fall day, but his back won't take it for more than a few minutes. He moves to the couch in the living room, but that's no good either. The pain is moving up from his lower back—L4 through L7, according to the X-ray tech—hand over hand like a malevolent gorilla. It will, he knows, end up swinging on his neck until his head throbs and white hot darts pierce his brain.

Your discs are disintegrating, he's been told. *Your spine must have been under some kind of extraordinary, regular stress as a child. Nothing we can do, really—you'll just have to learn to manage the pain.* One more jewel in the rich inheritance he's received from the Irish monster, to go along with the flashbacks, anxiety disorder, and the lesions. Gifts that keep on giving. *At least I'm not a drunk like he was.*

He moves back to the bedroom finally and, after throwing open the curtains, stretches out on the bed again. Gets up, restless; finds his backpack on the armchair to one side of the dresser, and brings it back to the bed. A small pack, the kind college kids wear—it doesn't pay to look homeless. Rooting through the socks and underwear, he finds a baggie with enough roaches in it to make up one more short joint. It'll help a little, but not a lot; he'll save it until later this afternoon when he really needs it.

It helps to know that Mario, bless him, has promised to bring back more crystal meth. He picks up the fragile glass pipe from the bedside table, waggles it longingly between his fingers. *I'll need it.*

My name is Colm—

LINDA

Finnegan watches her through the storm door, his wet nose blowing a fog patch on the glass. He's wagging his tail slowly, grinning at her with his tongue hanging out the side of his mouth. Looking hopeful still—no creature is more optimistic than a dog. Although he must by now sense, as she loads her gear through the side door of the van at the curb, that if he gets that walk he wants, it won't be from her. Not tonight.

A lovely fall evening and the first night of her hockey season. Just a weekly house league game at the local arena, but she has been anticipating it for a month. A couple of hours of escapism with a bunch of other women she barely knows. No burdens, relational or otherwise, just the sweet hissing slice of blades on ice, the echoing boom of the puck against the boards, the crisp snick of it hitting the stick on a hard pass. The pleasure of her own responsive body performing complex maneuvers at speed.

Maybe one of the girls will walk the dog. If not, Wayne will, once he has cuddled Marky awhile and put him to bed.

How simple that sounds, she thinks. Cuddling ought to be a way of slowing a child down, getting him ready for sleep, not a methodology for keeping him awake and therefore stimulated a little bit longer. Putting him to bed—at thirteen. With the girls it was a matter of banging on the bathroom door when they dawdled too long, negotiating a half-hour extension so they could finish watching some TV show, which, if missed, would stunt their social development for eons. But Marky is half the size he should be and three times the work.

He's a blessing, she tells God as she pulls away from the curb. *To us and lots of other people, too. It just takes so much effort to actually get the blessing …* Wayne will have to undress him, change his diaper, and fish his rubbery limbs through the sleeves and legs of his pajamas all while Marky lies there passively. That's a recent development: Until a month ago, he could still sit up on his own. Now his spine seems to have gone missing, and his head is likely to roll alarmingly backward on a neck newly disinterested in offering support.

Another marker of his decline. How she does hate to acknowledge them.

She remembers the high point, some five years ago now. At eight years of age, Marky walked unaided for the first time. Wayne, always more expressive than her, had been as jubilant as if his son had won the Boston Marathon. His boy was going to prove the doctors wrong! He fired off e-mails, wrote a family newsletter, made an announcement in church. Linda wasn't so sure, but how could you not be excited about it?

They had been away, just her and Wayne, for a weekend visit back to Montreal. A friend had come in to give respite care and watch the girls. She had jollied and coaxed Marky all weekend long, and on Sunday afternoon, while she and Lynn whooped encouragement, scarcely able to believe what they were seeing, he took twenty (that's right, two zero!) wobbling steps before collapsing in a beaming, burbling heap.

Linda has arrived at Moss Park Arena. She jockeys the van into an empty space, which is no mean feat in this tiny parking lot, and pauses a moment before getting her gear to see if there's anyone she knows in the small crowd on the wide boulevard at the corner or drifting through the park itself. Darkness has fallen, but the streetlights preserve a false dusk.

They were living in the north end of Scarborough then, on one of those streets where, if you weren't careful, you could end up parking your car in the neighbors' driveway and step through their front door before realizing that you'd missed your own place by two or three houses. A careful, sanitized neighborhood, where families kept their mess indoors.

If Marky had been their first, they probably wouldn't have even suspected anything was wrong before that routine visit to the GP one month after his birth. But Lynn and Erin had both been healthy, normal babies, so they weren't terribly surprised at the doctor's concern that he was sleeping such long stretches for a newborn and that his limbs were a little on the floppy side.

"Hmm," he'd said, waggling Marky's little leg thoughtfully. "Something's not quite right here...."

She'd not been surprised, but still it felt as if someone had clamped a clammy hand around her throat. And now, as she pulls her bag and sticks from the van, she feels it once again. She thinks about the new wheelchair that's on its way, a recliner, because Marky can no longer stay upright in his old chair, even when he's belted in. It's as if some evil elf slips into his room each night and magically removes one more bone from his little body.

The GP sent them to a pediatrician, who also declared that there was some kind of a problem and forwarded them to a neurologist, who hemmed and hawed and pushed his glasses back up the slope of his nose and ordered a slew of tests. *Few things*, she thought, *make a doctor, particularly a specialist, more uncomfortable than not knowing what's wrong.*

She and Wayne went for a walk when they got back from that visit. Not long, just around the block. But long enough to face the creeping realization that their little boy wouldn't throw a ball like other kids, run like other kids—maybe not even walk—certainly he'd never play hockey with his mom. That had been her secret dream. She had been so thrilled to have a boy. They were able to chuckle a little at that, that it was his mom, not his dad, who longed to teach him to skate, show him how to stick handle, overhear him bragging to his friends about his mom's wrist shot. NASCAR and motorcycles were more Wayne's line.

And then Wayne began to weep. Linda walked along beside him, rubbing a patch between his shoulder blades as if that was the source of his pain. But she didn't cry, not then. Didn't feel sad so much as hollow. And, she would later admit, angry. Familiar feelings, ones that had followed her for fifteen years, ever since her mother had died.

So much pain, generation after generation. She greets the other women in the locker room, a bunch she hasn't seen since last season and a few new faces. She chats briefly with a line mate from last year, then sits down, and zips open her bag.

Linda had been angry at her mother, her best friend, for leaving her when she was only seventeen. Angry that a simple gallbladder operation had revealed a raging cancer that chewed the life out of her in four short months. Angry that she had never been told about the cancer's first appearance six years earlier, that she spent her high school graduation in a funeral parlor. Angry that her father continued on as if on automatic pilot, as emotionally removed as ever. And angry that her brother, Peter, was not as devastated by their mother's death as she was. She didn't show the anger. Probably didn't even recognize then what it was. It kept her from sinking into a terrifying pit of sadness that yawned in a dark corner of her heart.

She had lost all four of her grandparents too, in the preceding few years. Nanny, her father's mother, would take her each week to the cemetery and let fourteen-year-old Linda drive the car slowly around the smooth paved roads that wound through it, after they had put fresh flowers on the graves of the two sons she had lost as children.

That story was little more than a curiosity to Linda at the time. Never having lost anyone close and finding it impossible to imagine her own father as a seven-year-old boy, it all seemed remote, unreal.

His family had gone on a picnic near the Ottawa River. Once the meal had been spread out and eaten, his parents stretched out on the grass while young Philip and his two older brothers snuck off for a swim. Nanny related the facts in the barest possible way: Her nine-year-old son began to struggle in the current, the eleven-year-old dove in to help him, and both were drowned. Philip found his way back to his parents and informed them that their two other sons were dead.

How strange is it that she is able to calmly recall all this, at forty-seven years of age, a year older than her mother was when she died, a year older than Peter was when he also died of cancer, while she laces up her skates and tapes her shin pads in place? Some other part of her is listening and responding to the banter of the other women while offering no clue as to what is really going on within her. How many of them are also here to find a brief reprieve from the weight of loss and disappointment in their lives? They all sound so cheerful, full of life. Their faces are flushed with anticipation, as if they are school-girls. *And I must look the same way to them.*

At forty, she fully expected to be dead by this age. To have sur-passed Peter and her mother … victory with a bitter aftertaste.

So much loss. And now losing their own little prince, Marky, an inch at a time.

They had no idea, when he staggered those twenty steps, that this was as good as it would get. After that, no matter how they encour-aged and coaxed him, as soon as they slipped their fingers from his up-reached hands, his legs would fold, and his bum would hit the floor. He could at least stay sitting upright then and would look momentarily stunned before beginning to giggle. Twenty steps. One time only, and she and Wayne never even got to see it.

And since then, the long, slow slide … they got him a walker and splints for his legs to try to build him back up to the point where he'd be able to walk alone again. Then a helmet, because he'd started to tumble from the walker. Seizures and more seizures, until his poor little head simply lolled in exhaustion between them, waiting for the next one to arrive. A constant fiddling with medications, trying to find that sweet spot where the seizures would stop, or at least slow down, and Marky wouldn't be doped into oblivion.

After awhile, he couldn't manage the walker; soon he couldn't even walk with them holding his hands. He'd just dangle there, his legs collapsing beneath him as they tried to encourage him to bear even a little of his own weight. A wheelchair, then. It was a relief to strap him into it and know that he was safe. He seemed happier too, burbling away, pushing Cheerios around on the tray in front of him and mashing the occasional one into his mouth.

But, at the same time, it was a sharp pain, like a long, narrow needle in her chest. Another incontrovertible marker of his increasing disability. One more declaration that her boy would never strap 'em on and hit the ice.

Odd, she thinks, as she steps through the gate and onto the ice herself, that this should be the place where her sorrow should choose to alight. It's not as if she's a fanatical player herself or that the game, in the larger scheme of things, matters to her very much at all. It's just a symbol, she guesses, of the thousand other losses, both tiny and large. She skates a stride or two, picks up a loose puck—half a dozen other women are already out here warming up—and pounds it against the sideboards. A satisfying "boom!" echoes around the rink.

A couple of years ago, they installed a chairlift on the stairs to the second floor. Marky is very small for his age, but certainly larger and heavier than an infant, and his muscle tone had deteriorated so much that it was like trying to carry forty pounds of wet spaghetti up those steep stairs. Not so bad in the morning, but by the end of the day when she was tired herself. A few times, she had almost dropped him. Wayne was great, absolutely devoted to Marky, but he couldn't always be around. Lynn and Erin had a harder time carrying him than Linda. The kicker: Something in the vibration of the lift almost invariably triggered a seizure. Hold him on the chair while he twitched and flopped, or carry him and risk tumbling him down the stairs?

Then, just before last Christmas, Marky had caught pneumonia. They almost lost him. His strength was so depleted, he'd begun to have trouble eating. Feeding him had always been a slow process, but now even pureed food couldn't make it past his tongue. And since his meds were mixed with his food, it meant the seizures were on the rise again.

So, the feeding tube. Like an extra plastic belly button, just above his fleshly one, about the size of a pencil. Pureed food and meds in an IV bag, pumped directly into his stomach. It's a three-hour process, but at least they know he's getting what he needs.

Wayne will just be unhooking him now and flushing the tube, she thinks as one of the women shouts that it's time to get the game under way. Light jerseys against dark. Linda counts five other women on her side who have already lined up for the face-off, and skates away. Sitting on the bench, she squirts some water through the cage on her helmet and rinses her mouth.

By the end of the day, Marky is so exhausted that trying to feed him orally is a physical impossibility. But Linda still tries in the morning, holding his head upright with one hand while scooping the rejected mush off his chin and shoveling it back between unresisting lips. Sometimes a little of it sneaks by his busy tongue, but it takes forever. Wayne thinks they should just tube feed him all the time, so that they know he's getting nutrients and the proper amount of medication.

Linda knows this makes sense, but something in her resists it. *There's no way back,* she thinks. *Once we stop feeding him orally, it will be like everything else—he'll never be able to start it up again. I don't want my son to stop eating food himself. It's just another step toward ...*

Her head snaps up as a teammate, arriving in a shower of snow, smacks the boards right in front of Linda with her stick. She's been in a daze; she leaps to her feet, scrambles for her gloves and stick, and leaps over the boards.

CHAPTER 12

SUFFERING AND GLORY

If we are suffering illness, poverty, or misfortune, we think we shall be
satisfied on the day it ceases. But there too, we know it is false; so soon
as one has got used to not suffering one wants something else.
—Simone Weil, Some Thoughts on the Love of God

Did not the Christ have to suffer these things and then enter his glory?
—Jesus, Luke 24:26

I was walking one day through Withrow Park, in Toronto's Riverdale
neighborhood, when, at the top of a long flight of stairs, I passed a young
woman who sat reading a book on a park bench. Although I didn't look
directly at her, it registered that she was young, severely dressed in a
quasi-Goth manner, and sitting rigidly upright. It's a strange place for
a park bench, right beside the head of a stairway. People using the stairs
must pass close to and directly in front of anyone sitting there. I had
never seen anyone use that bench before, nor have I since.

As I stepped past her, she looked up and asked if I had the time.

"Sure," I said, stopping and turning back toward her. I squinted at my
watch and, glancing at her, made my report. Then I went on my way.

It took perhaps twenty seconds to make sense of what I had seen. She was a normal-enough-looking young woman, perhaps twenty, with lovely pale skin, reddish hair with square-cut bangs that framed her face like an old-time helmet, and no-nonsense dark-rimmed glasses perched on a button nose. She wore a dress or blouse with a low neckline, cut as squarely as her bangs.

Because I had looked at her so briefly, I turned away at first thinking that the pink pattern that spread across the entire exposed area of her chest, something like a candelabra or a family tree in shape, was the outline of a tattoo to be filled in later. That alone would have bothered me. Whenever I see a young woman with a full-sleeve tattoo or extensive designs on her chest or neck, I can't help but think, *Oh, my dear, you'll be regretting that in twenty years ...*

But it wasn't just a tattoo. The pink lines glistened; they were about a quarter of an inch in width and distinctly raised from the rest of her clear, pale flesh. Halfway across the soccer field, I realized that she had been branded.

I thought about the fact that she had chosen such an odd, public place to sit and had stopped me when it was evident I would pass by without looking directly at her, and I wondered. Was she insisting on being looked at? Had she chosen that neckline because the burns were still tender or because she wanted to display them? Why would an apparently normal young woman submit herself to something so painful and disfiguring?

I have a tattoo myself. It's a lion and lamb, about the circumference of a tennis ball, on the inside of my right forearm. Having it done hurt no more than a mild sunburn, for which I was grateful. But I know that there are people who become addicted to getting tattoos and that, for many, the more painful it is to get one, the better they feel about that particular tat. I've read about and watched news reports on the growing number of people who engage in "extreme piercing," sometimes hanging from huge hooks that have been threaded through the muscles on their chests or backs or both. Some years ago in my own fair city, a local fringe magazine reported on a Halloween art piercing party, where one "artist" sewed his lips shut for the evening.

People who engage in these practices speak enthusiastically about the endorphin rush that accompanies the pain. Some will say that their bodies are instrument and supreme objet d'art—that art itself is worthless unless the artist suffers for it. Others will frankly admit that they are survivors of physical or sexual abuse; *that* suffering predisposed them to *this* suffering, but at least this suffering is one they have chosen themselves. For them, inflicting pain on themselves is a matter of regaining control over their own bodies; the scars and tattoos are the badges that declare that they have triumphed over their persecutors.

In the sexual realm, of course, the permutations of this sort of approach to the inescapable, universal reality of suffering are as varied as they are tawdry.

The truth is that, regardless of the tortuous spins we will put on it to try to convince ourselves that we are in control, suffering is one of the great human common denominators—rich, poor, weak, powerful, privileged, or excluded.

If you walked into the office at Sanctuary and met Linda, who is our office manager, you would have no immediate clue as to what she herself suffers or her family's history of loss. You might know her for years, as I have, and count her a close friend, as I do, and never think of her as "a great sufferer." Linda wouldn't think of herself that way either. And yet.

If you had met Colm during the period that his "portrait" describes, you might have recognized him as one who suffered more than most—if you had gotten to know him well enough to get past the facade he then worked so hard to maintain. He's come a long, long way since those days, I'm happy to say, facing the truth about his addictions, the abuses of his past, and his subsequent behavior. Now, you'd have to know him for quite a while before you began to realize that he has endured constant, extraordinary suffering from the time he was a little child, not because he's hiding it, but because he has experienced so much healing.

Both Linda and Colm are moving toward glory.

The suffering of many of my friends from the street is written large upon them. It is so pervasive in their lives that they cannot even afford the energy to pretend otherwise. This is what makes them appear so wretched and pitiful—and, if you look long and closely, so very, very beautiful.

My friend Norm Allen has for many years been a spiritual companion to a growing community of business leaders in Toronto. Most are, by any standard, very successful and quite wealthy. And yet, he tells me, "They have as much pain in their lives as your people." With the caveat that it's one thing to suffer when you have a house, a bed, and a full larder, and quite another to do so when you stuff your jacket with newspaper and curl up under a bridge at night, I agree with him.

Suffering is *the* great theological, philosophical problem.

"If there is a loving, just, and merciful God, why do innocent people suffer?"

"Do human beings require suffering to define their existence and qualify pleasure?"

"Is it possible to live without suffering or without causing others to suffer?"

As a Christian, the first of those questions concerns me most. I have tried, as seriously as I know how, to follow Jesus since I was in my early teens. I've studied Scripture diligently, read a smattering of theology and philosophy, and pondered the matter as deeply as I am able for almost my entire adult life.

I'm stumped.

Oh, I know the requisite theological equations. The most nearly applicable one in my situation, given my background, training, and inclination, goes like this:

God loves us and wants us to love him in return. True love cannot be commanded or preprogrammed but can only be freely offered. Free will for humanity is therefore a necessity. If any given human being is to be free to love, he or she must therefore also be free to hate; i.e., free to do good or to do evil. If a man or woman chooses to do evil, this will of necessity cause suffering in the world, even for people who are otherwise innocent. Ergo, all suffering in the world is humanity's own doing and a necessary result of the condition of our freedom to choose for or against God.

This is very tidy, virtually airtight if you come at it from the "right" angle. But, pardon me—it still sucks.

Whether this argument is the sum total of the absolute truth in the matter or (as many atheistic apologists will argue) a matter of his followers letting God off the hook, it's profoundly unsatisfying. I used to be content with this line of thinking when I was younger and had seen and experienced less suffering than I have now. I have such a privileged background that what little suffering I had endured I had largely caused myself. The equation, then, made sense.

But when I hear the stories of friends like Colm, and I've heard dozens of them, who *as toddlers* were abused sexually and physically by the very people who ought to have protected them, and who have lived their entire adult lives in great pain as a result, I find myself saying to God, "I get how this whole free will thing works. I can see how, in a mathematical sort of way, it was necessary for Colm's dad to have the freedom to choose to rape him when he was three years old. But I'm only human! You're God, and *you* ought to be able to figure out something better than this!"

If you get an inkling that I sometimes feel a little angry about this, well, you'd be spot on. God, fortunately, is gracious and unendingly patient with me and more than able to bear my little tantrums.

My friend Geoff Ryan is a Salvation Army officer who spent years in Chechnya during the revolution there and is now leading a church with his wife, Sandra, in one of Toronto's poorest neighborhoods. He says that when we ask, "Why is there suffering?" or some version of that question, we are simply asking the wrong thing. It's a fruitless question, like asking, "Why must a circle be round?" When we encounter suffering, Geoff says, we should be asking, "How should I respond to it?"[1]

This, I find, is a more fruitful line of thinking. Instead of trapping me in the anger sparked by being hurt or the living death of a victim mentality, it starts me thinking about the new kind of strength that emerges from healing and the possibility that resurrection—a new life—is not a remote concept to be enfleshed only at the end of time or a phenomenon so rare that it hasn't occurred in two thousand years.

(If you discount stories like the one about St. Denis, patron saint of Paris, who is said to have picked up his own head after having it lopped off by the Romans and walked to his own grave!) It gets me thinking about transcendence, the beauty of overcoming. In a word, it gets me thinking about glory.

Glory and suffering are inextricably linked.

This is true even in the most secular expressions of pop culture. The glory of any champion sports team is found in its capacity to overcome the obstacles presented by every other team between it and the trophy. Like Linda and most other Canadians, hockey is the team sport I love most. The Stanley Cup is the oldest trophy in professional sports, and the NHL playoffs are the longest and most grueling. Four best-of-seven rounds, a physically brutal game requiring at the same time incredible dexterity, played at such high speed that even the best players in the world can keep up the pace for only about forty-five seconds at a time. An absolute minimum of sixteen games, which I don't think has ever been done, a maximum of twenty-eight. If regulation time ends in a tie, the teams keep on playing until someone scores. Sometimes a playoff game will be twice the regular length—and a few times in history, a game begun at eight o'clock in the evening has ended in the wee hours of the morning.

"It's a war of attrition!" the announcers will crow, since, like most sports, bench strength is a major factor. Who will go down with an injury? Who will fade because he simply doesn't have enough stamina to sustain his game at such a high level for so long? Who will, by extraordinary skill and determination, overcome injury and fatigue, the suffering inflicted by the body checks, stick slashes, and even punches of the foe and emerge the victor? Skating around the ice surface with the three-foot high antique silver punch bowl, inscribed with the names of past winners, held triumphantly above his head while the crowd stands and bellows its adulation?

Glory ...

How about Lance Armstrong, a multiple champion already, but never more so than when he overcame cancer as well as the best riders in the world to win the Tour de France, probably the most demanding single competitor event there is?

Nobody, even the fans of the winner, really wants to see a blowout in a championship event. We thrill to the idea that the champ has been pushed to his or her absolute limit, that we have seen all they have to give, and that we may never see its like again.

We often apply the same standard in the world of art, reserving our deepest awe for those whose genius seems to be drawn from wells of pain and tragedy: Vincent Van Gogh, Kurt Cobain, Dylan Thomas, James Dean.

How about war, that absurd, tragic theater that reveals the worst and best of humanity? The medals we hold in highest honor are reserved for those soldiers who do battle with fear itself and are willing to risk pain, maiming, or even death for their mates. There are few things that move us more than a man who gives up his life for his friends.

Glory.

There is evidence of our hunger for glory even in the substitutes we seek for ourselves and respect in others. Fame, money, power, collegial respect—these measures of success are all about feeling that I have overcome, that I am on the top of the heap and that others are looking *up* to me.

My many friends who have no hope of gaining any of these more accepted standards of "glory" settle for lesser forms: a reputation as a sex worker who can command the highest dollar, a rounder who can defend his corner or park bench, the convict who is doing the hardest time because he's done the baddest crime. Or, simply, a drug or liquid that allows its user to transcend the cruel, abject, material, and spiritual poverty of his or her life and exult, even for a brief moment, in a state of euphoric rightness.

Tragically, the best many of my friends can hope for is to feel, for a short time, nothing at all.

The writer of Hebrews encourages us to "fix our eyes on Jesus, the author and perfecter of our faith, who for the joy set before him endured the cross, scorning its shame, and sat down at the right hand of the throne of God" (Heb. 12:2). That, he says, is how we should run the race too.

With apologies to those who choose to stitch their lips together or hang from meat hooks, you'd have to be crazy to actively seek suffering. Even Jesus didn't do that. Certainly he knew all about the suffering he would face and chose (although not easily; see Gethsemane) not to turn away from it, but he did so because he was focused on the joy he knew was on ahead. He knew that suffering was the price of glory.

The point, then, is not that we should choose suffering, unless perhaps it is the minimal kind involved in disciplining the body to some higher purpose—fasting, for instance, or physical training. There's more than enough suffering in the world already. (Say "amen," somebody!)

The question I face is, as Geoff says, "What will I do with the suffering I encounter in my own life and in the lives of others around me?" Will I run from it? Avert my eyes? Stuff it down inside me, put a lid on it, and pretend that it is not affecting me? Rant and rave at the injustice of it? Blame God, my parents, the government, the church, or some version of "them"?

Jesus is the Way I choose to follow, and his way is the way of the cross. "Pick up yours," he says, "and follow me" (see Matt. 16:24). Suffering is unavoidable and the only road to glory. Expressions of this abound in the Bible, but the most cogent comes from the lips of Jesus, after his resurrection, when he explained to the puzzled pair on the Emmaus road, "Did not the Christ *have* to suffer these things and *then* enter his glory?" (Luke 24:26).

I am so glad I don't have to walk this road alone. I am surrounded by companions, both rich and poor, who struggle in the same ways I do; and I am learning to both lean on them and lend what strength I have to them. I am even told that a "great cloud of witnesses" who have run this marathon before, finished it, and are in the stands, watching, cheering me and my mates on (Heb. 12:1).

People who roam the back alleys and people who occupy the office towers or suburban back-splits may appear to cope with life's disappointments in different ways, but up close they look remarkably similar. Together, we are learning to embrace the difficult stuff on the journey and grow from it, instead of trying to avoid it, cover it up, or pretend it's not there.

We are moving from investing our energy in *anger*, or other forms of avoidance, which are destructive, and toward *sorrow*—at first a frightening, but ultimately a healing path.

We rise up from the powerless prostration of the many *deaths*, both small and great, that we die and glory in both the hope and the present reality of *resurrection*.

That glow on the horizon grows brighter as we draw closer.

CHAPTER 13

FROM ANGER TO SORROW

Then the LORD *said to Cain, "Why are you angry? …*
Sin is crouching at your door; it desires to have you."
—*Genesis 4:6–7*

He is despised and rejected of men; a man
of sorrows, and acquainted with grief.
—*Isaiah 53:3* KJV

Larry was lying on the bed, waiting for Shelley to come back with some food, when he heard the thump on the floor above him. Later, he wasn't sure what made him move—thumps weren't exactly uncommon in the rooming house on Charles Street. Neither was loud cursing, a fistfight in the hallway, a cracker banging on your door at three a.m., or the whine of police sirens. Still, something told him: *Go have a look. Now.*

He rolled off the bed and onto his feet, grabbed an empty beer bottle by the neck, and took off down the corridor and up the stairs.

As he rounded the head of the stairway, he could see down the length of the hallway. There at the end of it, he saw Brett, another resident, in a kind of half crouch, bending over an indistinguishable pile

179

on the floor. Larry sprinted down the corridor toward him. As Larry skidded to a halt a few yards away, Brett straightened up and turned to look at Larry. He seemed dazed, as if he couldn't quite believe that he'd woken up and found himself in this particular spot.

After a long empty second, Brett spoke. "You better call 911."

Then he dropped the knife on the body at his feet, pushed past Larry, and ran.

When I passed the place the next morning, on my way to Sanctuary, there were three or four cruisers outside and a cop leaning against the wall beside the entrance. I knew a lot of the residents there at the time, so once I had dumped my gear and locked up my bike, I wandered back to find out what was going on.

"Somebody in there got shanked!" a guy in a winter jacket with the insulation spilling from rips on the shoulders and sleeves announced.

The officer outside and all but one of the cruisers had disappeared, so I entered and poked around until I found the scene of the crime. It was hard to miss. I looked down the end of a long hallway with walls that were once pale green, punctuated at rigorous intervals by maroon doors bearing consecutive numbers written in Magic Marker. The section right in front of the door to the communal bathroom was cordoned off with yellow police tape. A police officer stood blocking the entrance, his hands folded primly before him, regarding me with a pale stare. On the floor, I saw the chalked outline of a body and the proverbial pool of blood.

The officer didn't know who the victim was or who had done the deed and didn't seem much interested. Thought the vic had probably been taken to St. Mike's, but that was last night before he came on duty, and anyway, he was just there to guard the scene.

I went outside and found Larry having a smoke, inspecting the patch of sidewalk between his feet. Larry was no softie; he'd seen a thing or two, but when I called his name, he looked up with wide eyes staring out of an abnormally pale face.

It was Kirk, he said. They'd been operating on him all night. He was alive, but ... Larry had finally come home to try to get some sleep. The cops had Brett already—he had run from the building, but after that he apparently just plopped down on a park bench half a block away and waited for the cops to find him. Larry still couldn't believe it.

When I told the ICU nurse I was Kirk's pastor, she took me straight in to his bedside. Nobody else had come asking after him once Larry had left, and they had no information about anybody else who should be notified. I said nothing but wondered if his girlfriend, Trina, knew yet.

Kirk was stretched out, straight and stiff as if at attention, on a bed tilted up at the head. One light sheet covered him from the waist down. The rest of him sprouted a wild garden of tubes and hoses, but for the wide, thick swath of surgical pad running from the base of his throat to south of his belly button. There was bright blood seeping through it already. Despite the rise and fall of his chest, to the metronomic click of the pump that filled and emptied his lungs, he was gray and still as if the bed was his cooling board and he just waiting for the hearse to arrive.

Careful not to disturb the instrument clamped on his finger, I took his hand and squeezed. Spoke his name, directly into his ear. Prayed for him. No response.

I stayed quite awhile, watching the abrupt rise and slow fall of his chest. A nurse bustled in and out every ten minutes or so, peering closely at a couple of monitors and bending to give a tube that came from under the sheet and hung by the side of the bed a flick with her finger. She rarely looked at Kirk at all and politely declined to discuss his chances, saying I'd better talk to the surgeon. When he showed up—a surprisingly young and far-too-weary man—he explained to me that, although Kirk had been stabbed from behind, they'd had to open him up from the front and spread his rib cage wide in order to get at the damage. He was being kept in an induced coma to reduce the likelihood of reopening his wounds.

"There were three punctures," he reported flatly. "One missed anything important, but one nicked his kidney, and the other put a hole in his heart. If his friend hadn't called 911 when he did …"

When I asked him what the prognosis was, he looked at me for a moment, opened his mouth, closed it, and shrugged.

Trina finally showed up when I was visiting a few days later. She had been on an extended crack run since she'd heard and was a mess. There were little black streams running down her cheeks from her mascaraed eyes even before she showed up, but when she saw him, her eyes burst into full flow. She turned and ran from the unit, trying to stuff the sobs back into her mouth with both hands.

They were a truly toxic pair, Kirk and Trina, but I liked both of them a lot. Still do. She could gain or lose thirty pounds in a matter of a couple of weeks. Even when she wasn't working, just walking along any old street in a pair of baggy sweats, a car would pull over, and the driver would lean out and ask how much. It wasn't that she was gorgeous—she could and usually did look great when she was rested and all done up, but just as often in those days she looked like a train wreck. There was just something about her, as if she were sending out a signal only johns could hear. It was handy when she was working, but a pain when she wasn't.

Kirk was cocky and abrasive and strutted around like someone had stuck a firecracker up his fluke. I was one of many who sometimes wanted to. He wore a long blond mullet and held his arms out a little as if his muscles were too big to let them rest at his sides. He was a scrapper and a bully, constantly indignant at slights, injustices, and misfortunes, both real and imagined. He was cranky when he was straight, dangerous when he was stoned.

Kirk and Trina's relationship was in constant crisis. He said he didn't want her out working the streets, but he couldn't wait for her to get home with the crack. She claimed she wanted only him but seemed often to go out prostituting merely out of boredom, sometimes disappearing for days at a time. Maybe she just needed time away from him.

They fought and bickered and complained about each other constantly. Kirk was often charming, and although I never saw him lay a hand on her, his anger could be sparked by anything at all. They often ended up yelling at each other across the room in our drop-ins. Other people would roll their eyes—*there they go again.* Our staff would sigh, get between them, and insist they take it outside. Off they'd go down the street, on opposite sidewalks, spouting threats and insults.

I didn't know what had set Brett off, but I could imagine Kirk jacking him up for his crack when the mood struck, threatening him because he'd closed the door to his adjoining room too loud or shoving him out of the way when they passed in the corridor. Probably made fun of him in front of other people, too, since Brett was a quirky, weedy character. I had never known him to even threaten anyone before.

It was about a week before Kirk came out of the coma. He was understandably meek and quite emotional about the fact that I had kept coming to see him.

"I knew you were there, you know," he told me. "When you came and held my hand and talked to me? I don't remember anything else, but I remember that."

That was a God thing, I responded. I went over how lucky he was to be alive—if Larry hadn't mysteriously known something was up; if he had lain there a minute or two before coming to investigate; if Brett had shoved just a little harder or a half inch higher; if Larry had wasted time trying to revive him instead of running for the phone right away; if the ambulance station had been just a little farther away; if the surgeon hadn't been right there when he was wheeled in…

I'll admit I was a little heavy handed, but I was thinking, *God, if you can't reel this guy in now, you never will.*

Kirk nodded and cried a little, gently touching the row of bright ferocious staples that marched the length of his torso with his fingertips. He asked about Trina. I told him about her one visit and that she hadn't been back. He nodded again, unsurprised. She'd show up eventually. Things would be different now, he proclaimed with as much vehemence as his tender chest would allow. This was a warning to him; God had been looking out for him, and he was going to quit the crack and all the other street nonsense.

When I saw him next, a few days later, he was looking a little perkier. Trina had been in. He'd set her straight, he said: They were going to get things under control.

I asked him about the police. Had the detectives been in to see him yet?

His eyes bugged out. He clenched his teeth and growled. He wasn't talking to them. He was no rat. Besides, he was going to get the little b— himself. Not right away. Heal up first, let him sweat and keep looking over his shoulder for a year or so. Even then he wouldn't kill him, at least not first thing, just beat the living crap out of him every time their paths crossed. And Kirk would make sure their paths crossed often.

Oh boy, I thought.

Kirk spent about three weeks in the hospital before moving back into the room in the house on Charles Street. Brett was in custody, but Kirk wouldn't give the cops anything, claiming that because the assailant had attacked him from behind, he was never able to identify who it was. The detectives would sigh, cock an eyebrow at him—they knew this game, knew that the worst thing you can be on the street is a rat, knew that a bad guy like Kirk would favor vengeance over the vagaries of the justice system. They had come back a few more times, changing their angle of approach, but Kirk just ground his teeth and spat out the same response.

Brett was denied bail and spent a long time in detention, but he never did come to trial. With only Larry's testimony, and he wasn't much more enthusiastic about taking the stand than Kirk, the police figured they would get an aggravated assault conviction at best. By the time they dropped the charges and let Brett go, he had done enough "dead time" at the Don Jail that he'd be released on the basis of time served anyway. ("Dead time" is twenty-three hours [minimum] per day in presentencing detention lockup. The Don was so crowded and in such shambles that judges routinely awarded dead time served there against someone's sentence at a rate of three days for one.)

Kirk and Trina managed to do well for a couple of weeks after he got out of the hospital. Kirk lay on the bed in their tiny room, trying not to moan, popping painkillers. Trina fed him soup, fussed over his pillows, and held his elbow when he went for short, shuffling walks. It might have been the nearest thing to domestic bliss they had ever experienced.

It all unraveled pretty quickly. The stronger Kirk felt, the angrier he got. He'd lie there, looking at the staples—it looked like there was an industrial strength zipper sewn into his hide—and plan an ever-fuller range of sorrows and indignities to be bestowed on Brett.

He barked at Trina: The soup was too hot, not hot enough; it was the same crap as the last three days, not as good as what he'd had yesterday; the painkillers weren't working (in an accusatory tone, as if it was her fault he didn't have something more effective). Why did she have garbage bags full of clothing she had cadged here and there, but had never worn, in every corner of the room? Couldn't she get those crackheads across the hall to keep it down a little? They'd been raving all night.

She barked back. She got all tarted up and went out to turn a few tricks, mostly because she knew that it would bug him and that he couldn't do a thing about it, but also because she needed some relief. She smoked the crack she bought before coming back to the room. A lot of her clients were rock stars anyway, and using with them was all part of the game. When she'd return, Kirk would take note of her red-rimmed eyes and hyper body language, but uncharacteristically, he'd say nothing.

One evening, as she was pulling on her high stiletto-heeled boots, he quietly said, "Bring some back."

They blew the next month's rent money on crack, which Kirk

justified because he was so uncomfortable staying in that particular room and seeing the stain on the floor just ten feet away.

I lost track of them from there. They headed farther downtown. They split up. Kirk or Trina sightings became like catching a glimpse of Elvis. Our staff would go looking for them late at night. The other shadows drifting around those dark streets would respond to our questions with shrugs or occasionally, "Yeah, he was around here half an hour ago, but I don't know where he went. Hey, could you spare a couple of bucks?"

One bright midday, I was driving past Filmore's, an ancient strip club and flophouse anchored at the corner of Dundas and George streets, where hookers and addicts go marching in two by two but come out alone. Half-a-dozen local entrepreneurs lounged against the long blank wall that borders Dundas. Kirk was one of them.

I wheeled the battered old Chevy van over to the curb, wound down the passenger window, and called his name. In the side mirror, I saw him look suspiciously at the van and, when I called his name again, crab walk reluctantly in my direction. He stayed a good three or four feet away from the passenger door, bending down a bit to peer through the interior gloom at me.

Recognizing who it was, his face brightened. He lunged toward the door and stuck his arm through the window to shake my hand. We babbled happily at each other for a minute, then he turned and shouted to the other men who were watching curiously.

"Hey! Hey, guys! C'mere! Come and meet my pastor."

Well, that gave them pause. "Pastor" is not a term I chose for myself. I'm too keenly aware of the artificial ways in which it sets one apart from other people, engendering either an unwarranted

respect or, more often, a mild, suspicious repulsion—particularly
from addicts and dealers lounging outside a strip club. Kirk's mates
approached reluctantly, one by one, reached through the window to
shake my hand, then faded back to their stations at the wall.

Kirk looked pretty bad. He'd lost weight and muscle; his eyelids
were red, his skin still grayish. He'd always strutted around with his
chest out and shoulders thrown back, but now, he was hunched, his
shoulders drawn inward to protect a chest that was still obviously very
tender. He still had that bitter edge and fire in his eyes.

He told me, much later, that the staples had to stay for another
year—there are a couple still in there—because the incision healed so
slowly; it continued to weep and require bandaging for a year after
that. His constant crack use kept it from healing.

I saw him once more on the street, this time late at night and in
the "Crack Central" area where my staff mates and I had gone looking for him so often before. He had looked bad when I'd seen him at
Filmore's, but this time he looked only a few steps away from dying. He
was shrunken, hollow-eyed, and he'd gone all tizic.

Streetlights are sparse on that stretch of street, and a couple of res-
taurants had been boarded up, so when I called his name, he squinted
at me and twitched a little closer. Kirk had been humming and talking
to himself; when he recognized me and my outreach partner, he burst
into tears. Sobbing, he took a step toward us, faltered, and backed
away with a hand held up to ward us off. His back bumped against a
wrought iron fence sealing off an alleyway between two buildings, and
he came to a standstill.

We moved toward him, speaking quietly to try to calm him down.
He tried to talk, but the tears were pouring down his face, his nose

was running like a tap, and what words he managed to form made no sense. Nothing we said seemed to improve matters. After only a few minutes, he spun himself away from the fence, holding both palms out toward us, and backed away. After taking half-a-dozen steps like that, he turned and bolted, weeping furiously.

I didn't see him again for a long time. To be honest, I gave him up. If you had asked me to identify the one person I knew who I was sure would never get off the streets, it would have been Kirk.

Six or seven months later, I got a phone call. It was Kirk, and he sounded very, very different. He had been in a rehab program for months, he said, and still was. He had gotten far enough along that he was now allowed unescorted absences to meet with healthy friends and others who could help him in his recovery. He wanted to meet with his "pastor."

"They tell me in the program that only one person in twenty is still clean and sober after five years," he said when we met, looking relaxed and cheerful. "There are twenty of us in the program. I intend to be the one."

He's the one. Seven or eight years on, still clean and sober, he has marched steadily over or around every obstacle in his way. Recovery, he says, is 10 percent program and 90 percent God. Aggressiveness has turned to enthusiasm. The cocky strut is a jubilant stride. He's an exuberant, evangelical Jesus person, employed for several years now at a downtown mission, where he cares for the next wave of Kirks.

Some time ago, I sat down with both Kirk and Brett. He had heard that Kirk had changed, but having had the old Kirk catch up with him once or twice before he got sober, Brett wanted to make sure. He had asked me to see if I could get them together; having become a Christian too and having stepped away from his old habits, he was clean, healthy, and handsome.

To an outside observer, there would have been nothing dramatic about the meeting—three men on the patio of a coffee shop, talking quietly. But when we walked away, the old scores had all been settled, the skeletons laid to rest. No anger. Just the faint, dull ache of an old wound momentarily disturbed. Peace.

$ $ $

I don't know what fueled Kirk's abiding anger—it ruled him long before Brett ever stabbed him. I've never asked him, and I won't. I do know that he had begun using drugs and alcohol heavily by the time he was in his late teens and that he never mentions his parents or siblings—an omission that, in my experience, tells its own story.

Colm's thirty-five-year path of self-destruction began because of an eminently justified anger at his father, who abused him so mercilessly, and his mother, who watched it happen. She did nothing to stop it; instead, when he began to act out, she blamed him for causing trouble in the family and beat him. He became trapped by consecutive addictions, trading one substance for another, by self-deception, repeated job loss, years of homelessness, and actions that piled shame upon shame. His resentment exacerbated the physical damage that had been done to his body, his anxiety disorder, and his tendency to view others as either threats to his safety or tools to provide relief to his constant torment, or both.

Even Linda, who has all along lived such an apparently normal, healthy life, freely admits she spent many years angry at her mother, her father, her brother, and God. Her anger, as long as she cultivated it, steered her away from intimacy and any real hope of healing.

But Kirk, Colm, and Linda have come to realize that anger is a billowing flag planted in the fertile soil of loss and grief. As long as they fought to defend that flag, they continued to receive wound after debilitating wound. When, instead, they threw down that dark banner, knelt in the dirt, scooped it up, and let it flow through their fingers, they began to heal. The clamor of war gave way to weeping; their sorrow drew others to them instead of driving them off.

Anger is addictive because it makes me feel strong. It makes me believe that "I am right!" and that being right is what matters most. It builds a wall that, I desperately hope, will keep the marauder out. It becomes so intoxicating that I am constantly primed and ready to get some more and sends me strutting self-righteously down the street, head held high and heart beating double time. I may even come to the point of believing that I can't live without it. But anger only begets more anger, as violence begets violence. My tolerance to it increases; a little is too much, and a lot is never enough.

Anger, it must be admitted, is in its genesis both natural and useful, much like pain. When I see that flag flying, it warns me that I have been wounded. Once I have recognized that, I know that I must not keep my eyes fixed upon it, but let my hand slide down the flagpole until it rests in the dirt in which it is grounded.

Sorrow, as painful and frightening as it is, lasts only for a time. Sobbing turns to gentle tears, the tears dry, the gaping wound slowly closes. Soon it is only a dull ache forgotten for longer and longer periods of time, returning only now and then to remind me of how precious and costly true glory is.

The extremity of their poverty has made my friends inspiring and trustworthy guides on my own journey. Like Linda, the resources I

have inherited are so great that I can usually hide the more overt evi-
dences of the many secret wounds my own anger inflicts. But when
I witness brothers like Kirk and Colm driven to their knees by the
sheer weight of it—when I see them break and weep and then begin
to heal—it encourages me to be honest about the quieter addictions I
jealously protect.

They give me courage, these heroic companions, to abandon the
falsely bright security of my anger and walk toward the daunting but
true safety of genuine sorrow.

CHAPTER 14

FROM DEATH TO RESURRECTION

When Christ calls a man, he bids him come and die.
—*Dietrich Bonhoeffer,* The Cost of Discipleship

I am the resurrection and the life. He who believes
in me will live, even though he dies.
—*Jesus, John 11:25*

"Sunny California" was what the headline called her, and the large color photograph just below the fold made it obvious why. She could have been a model in a sportswear catalog: waves of golden hair spilling over her slender shoulders, a cupid's bow mouth curved in a smile, sparkling blue eyes. The red jersey she wore just added to the vibrancy she radiated, even in a blurry newspaper print.

Her friends in the Sanctuary community called her California, or just "Cali." There weren't many of us who even knew her real name. I had certified copies of her birth certificate and had written a letter of reference regarding some other government document a couple of years earlier but had long since forgotten all that by the time her picture hit the papers. Whatever name you offer, on the streets—that's who you are.

The image was an old one, taken years earlier during the time she actually lived in the state that had given her that tag, and so it didn't capture the toll a few years of street life had taken. She had gotten skinny and a little stooped—she was naturally a tall, graceful girl. Her skin had lost that glow. The smile was still there, but gentle now instead of brilliant, tamer, a weary smile that knew more than it wanted to.

Still, the picture in the paper was a good representation of the image most of us held of who Cali really was—her essential beauty, grace, sweetness, sense of style. She could stroll into the donated clothing room at one end of Sanctuary's drop-in room, rifle through a pile of picked-over castoffs, and emerge a few minutes later looking ready for the runway.

Some of our folks saw the yellow police tape and a couple of investigators when they arrived by subway for worship on Sunday evening. They wondered, battled that sinking feeling: *Not another one ...* The police said it was a woman but wouldn't say who or what exactly had happened. But California had gone missing late Saturday night.

A cop finally gave a name to a street guy who had the nerve to pester him, saying, "If she's one of ours, you gotta tell us. We might be the only family she has." The street guy wasn't sure it was her, since he had only known her by her street tag, but he knew that three of her friends had been staving off a horrifying, rising certainty for almost twenty-four interminable hours. The name he brought back late Sunday night, her real name, confirmed it.

On Monday morning, the news spread on the street like a grass fire. Her friends gathered by some mysterious instinct out front of Sanctuary or in the parkette next door, drawn out of the ravines and alleyways as if by the tolling of a mission bell only they could hear.

We all wept; many wailed and cried out. *Why her? Why now, just as she was beginning to get herself together? She was so sweet, so vulnerable. She never did anybody wrong—why her and not me?* Questions like that may sound melodramatic, archetypal. But the extraordinary thing here was that the people responding with such overt anguish were not unfamiliar with loss or violent death. Their usual response was grim impassivity, a slinking withdrawal from public view, and the anesthetizing of any feeling at all with drugs or booze. Cali's death touched a set of strings drawn to breaking point and sent a darkling chord thrumming through our community.

Cali's boyfriend, Brian, tortured himself: He had been only a block or two away when she was dying; why hadn't he been with her? Why hadn't he sensed something was wrong? He should have been there; he should have defended her. All manner of impossible things he required of himself and so grew wilder in his grief and pain.

So many questions and never an answer.

The news got worse. That Tuesday-morning article, with Cali's bright visage attached, informed the world that Toronto Transit Commission security cameras had caught an image of her descending the subway stairs with a young man. Twenty minutes later, the same cameras recorded him leaving with Cali's handbag over his shoulder. He had beaten her to death. Brian and others recognized the guy from the grainy pictures in the paper, but nobody really knew him—he came from uptown somewhere, wasn't a regular of the street scene.

We tried to comfort each other. Leila and Seven were Brian and Cali's neighbors down in the valley; their squats were within shouting distance of each other. They'd share canned food they had stored up and fall asleep listening to each other's occasional squabbling. Leila and

Seven put their arms around Brian and tried to hold him together as he swung from lengthy crying jags to short storms of vengeful intent. Such public emotion is considered weakness on the street, and weakness simply cannot be afforded in an environment that is so often about the survival of the meanest. Still, a wider and wider circle of Cali's friends gathered, weeping openly and at length, trying periodically but with little success to stuff the tears back down.

On Wednesday, the police announced that the accused had turned himself in. His family had seen his picture in the papers and on TV and had persuaded him to do the right thing. They, too, of course, were devastated. They had left their South American home to begin a new life in a country where their children would not be subjected to such a culture of violence. The killer was a young man, around twenty. And he'd recently been declared permanently unable to work because of brain damage resulting from an encounter with school-yard bullies here in Toronto.

Brian talked about doing crime, getting himself arrested and incarcerated, so that maybe he could get next to the guy who had stolen Cali from him. Seven and Leila hung on tight.

Our lunchtime drop-in that day and the suppertime drop-in the next night were a hurricane of emotions. Brian sat on the floor with his back against the wall, looking like someone had whacked him with a hammer between the eyes. Leila pinballed around the room, fractured and frantic. Seven disappeared.

Most of our staff members were on the ropes too. Sensing that, Brian, Leila, and others who had been close to Cali welcomed us into their circle of grief. We hugged each other and cried together in unprecedented fashion. Leila is pretty skittish around most men, but she sat beside Lyf, our actor in residence and a pastor in the community, and sobbed freely. We took some comfort in agreeing that the newspaper article had been pretty good—it had described Cali as a real person, with dignity, not as some lost waif who had died a sordid death.

Cali's connection with Sanctuary had been mentioned in the paper, and a couple of our staff had been interviewed, and so her mother tracked down our phone number and called. Cali had been in touch with her in recent months, she said, and making plans to come home. She had talked about going into rehab to get some help with her addiction and about getting a job, maybe returning to the catering work she had done years earlier. That agreed with what Cali had been saying to Keren, Thea, and Alan on our staff; and somehow it made it even harder to lose her.

Cali's mom was glad to hear that we were planning a memorial for her. She didn't think she and Cali's dad would be able to attend, though, but they were planning a small, very private funeral. I could understand it. Hard enough to lose your only daughter, harder still to be tortured by imagining what had happened to her. And how much harder to grieve all that while surrounded by the frightening and foreign people among whom her little girl had ended up living these last few years? She graciously sent photos of her daughter for us to use at the memorial and a brief, heartbreaking note to be read.

Cali's death felt like perhaps the biggest single loss our community had ever sustained. She hadn't been a hard-core street person—it seemed more like she had lost her way and had the immediate intention of climbing out of the hole she found herself in. She was a truly lovely, sweet-natured person, maintaining that character even in the midst of an environment that quickly hardens most people.

The men and women who make up Sanctuary's staff are far from callous, but neither are they naive. While I don't suppose you ever get used to losing people you have come to love, it is for us at least a familiar experience. We had lost, by my count, at least six people from our community in the twelve months before Cali's death, from the usual litany of causes—murder, suicide, overdose, the cumulative effects of street life, as well as "normal" things like cancer. All in all, it left us feeling pretty grim.

It was hard to see it at the time, but even in the midst of so much death, there was new life stirring. Following the Thursday night drop-in after California's death, the staff members who had been "on" that night gathered, as we usually do, to debrief. We were emotionally exhausted, beaten down, overwhelmed by grief, anger, and despair.

Plopping ourselves into the chairs in our little meeting room, we stared at each other dumbly. After a few minutes punctuated mainly by long sighs and disjointed chatter, we agreed on what we needed. Someone went to a nearby twenty-four-hour convenience store for bread. I fetched candles, a couple of glasses, and a bottle of port from my office.

We shared Communion together—and "communion," in my experience, has rarely been a more apt word. The brokenness of that bread stood for shattered lives in our community, the aching sense of loss and being lost that tore at our own hearts, our profound failure, we felt, to make a difference. It told us too, that Jesus was right there in our midst and out walking around in our neighborhood among our friends who, like us, were desperately trying to find a way to ease the pain.

But it didn't *feel* like he was there. I think we felt in that moment like Martha and Mary must have, after they had sent an urgent message about their sick brother Lazarus to Jesus: "Come quickly; the one you love is dying." And he stayed two more days in the distant town where he was when the message had first arrived. Waiting. Dawdling, apparently, while their own dear brother moaned and faded and finally expired. Easy enough to say, after the fact, that it was all just preparation for the resurrection that was coming, but what comfort was that at the time? Slim comfort, too, that he was "out there," seemingly doing nothing to change the courses of our friends who were actively seeking their own demise, doing nothing to protect those who, like Cali, were defenseless.

The wine: a deep, foreboding purplish red in the candlelight. Salvation, cleansing, healing. Words, mere words. But with the cup, a subtle shift. We must, we began to say to each other, recount the victories we have witnessed in the past. We must lift up our heads, look for whatever flickers of light we can spot in this present darkness, and place our hope in a dawn yet to be revealed. This, here and now, is what faith is. The only alternative is despair.

And so we did. For two hours, long after the bread and wine were gone, until the tea lights began to gutter, we told each other the stories we already knew. Little victories, most of them, and some of the eleventh-hour variety. Others that were a work in progress: people who had for years haunted the perimeter of the community but were now moving inward, giving and receiving care with a vulnerability we found amazing when we stopped to think about it. Stories like Kirk's, which had unfolded over such a long period of time that we had taken for granted the miracles that had taken place. We marveled at how frequently the greatest healing seemed to occur in the most hopeless cases and at how little we ourselves had to do with effecting it. These were not our victories—hardly ever could we point at actions we had taken to bring about the positive results we witnessed. It was God stuff; he was, after all, present and active.

Eyes glistened in the candlelight, and we didn't know if it was grief or joy—for this is the great advantage joy has over happiness: It can grow in the same soil as grief and even flourish.

California's memorial, a week later, was an amazing affair.

The news coverage of her death had alerted friends who had known her in her prestreet days. A buzz went around Facebook and other Internet chat networks. Although it was apparently not as fast as the grapevine on the street, it was considerably broader. High school friends, work colleagues, former roommates, and old family friends began to call Sanctuary, at first to confirm that it was the California they had known (her real name had been published in the newspaper and television accounts) and then to find out when the memorial would be.

It seems she had been as well loved in her previous life as she had become on the streets. More than a hundred people showed up, many of them bearing photographs, poems they had written about her, or other mementos. Perhaps the most touching was the bouquet that lay in front of Cali's photograph during the memorial. Another woman who has lived on the street for many years showed up at Sanctuary the day before and handed fifty dollars to Linda. I don't even want to know how she managed to get her hands on that much money. "Buy something nice for California," she said, all tizic and sodden with tears. Then she fled.

A regular feature of memorials in our community is the invitation to anyone so inclined to offer a memory of the person who has passed.

About a dozen people did so. Only a couple of those were friends from Cali's last few years on the street, and they were still too wrecked by shock and grief to offer much more than a few broken words and a fresh flood of tears.

But friends from her more distant past and a couple of relatives offered memories of happier times, and we received the precious gift of a fuller picture of her life, one that included more joy than sorrow.

Most of our own community members find memorials too hard—they have suffered so many losses, they have not learned to embrace sorrow, and often they can see too clearly in the passing of their friend an omen of their own imminent death. Leila, Seven, and Brian were present, although they had to come and go as emotions overcame them, but only a few others of her friends from the street found it possible to attend. I knew that there would be dozens more out on the streets somewhere, knowing the memorial was under way at Sanctuary, present in their hearts, but remembering her in their own fashion.

Meanwhile, out of sight and right in the midst of so much death and despair, a remarkable resurrection was taking place. I don't know that the members of our staff were even aware that Priscilla and Gerald had a close relationship with California—in fact, maybe they didn't. Maybe just sharing the same turf, living out their lives, more or less, within the same half-dozen city blocks, was enough of a connection.

Frankly, they weren't the ones we thought would be most deeply affected by Cali's murder. I've known both of them for years. Must have been a decade ago that Priscilla first showed up: a tall, slender "Indian Princess" with a husky voice and those classic, impossibly high Ojibwa cheekbones. She was charming, sometimes a little flirtatious, and tough as nails. She had two sisters, one of them transgendered, and a brother—all of them have spent years bouncing back and forth between jail and the street.

Despite the charm, Priscilla had a nasty edge. The years and bearing a few children had thickened her somewhat; now in her late twenties, she ruled the distaff side of the street. Unless her older sister Trish happened to be out of jail, she was, hands down, the meanest woman street fighter out there. She terrorized the other women, robbing them at will, and did the same to more than a few of the men. The fact that she had borne her children while homeless and quickly lost them to the Children's Aid Society did nothing to soften her. The kids had been placed with various family members, but Priscilla was so immersed in the alcohol, drugs, and violence of street life that she seemed to rarely spare them a thought.

Gerald is Cree. Tall, broad shouldered, with a wide pleasant face. He's nearsighted. On the odd occasion when I've seen him actually wearing glasses, he has a quiet, studious look, which is not far off his natural character. Gentle and soft-spoken when he's sober, he often became a vicious thug when he was drunk. I had watched it develop over the space of years. I was mildly surprised when I first heard that he'd gotten into a couple of scraps; he didn't seem the type, back then, but that's street life. Sometimes it comes to you whether you're looking for it or not. It didn't surprise me to hear that he'd taken the worst of it.

It didn't cow him, though. It made him tougher, meaner. Every time I heard about him getting into a fight after that, his reputation grew a little. Came a time when he started the scraps—nobody wanted to start one with him anymore—and ended them too, with a regularity and violence that were unsettling. There often seemed to be no real reason for a particular fight, not even the ridiculous kind of beef so common on the street. He just seemed to be getting angrier and angrier.

Thea and Keren reported to the rest of the staff that people were showing up regularly in the clinic, bearing wounds and bruises inflicted on them by Priscilla or Gerald. Then they hooked up together, and you could almost feel the street shudder.

It was a strange romance, a Bonnie-and-Clyde sort of thing, but lacking the flivvers, tommy guns, and double-breasted suits. They robbed other homeless or street-involved people, instead of banks, with an escalating brutality and randomness. When they couldn't find someone else to beat up, they'd whale away on each other. They'd make the superhuman effort to get off the streets and get an apartment—and lose it a month or two later. Gerald would decide he wanted to get sober; Priscilla would laugh in his face, say humiliating things, and slap him around. A few weeks later, it would be Priscilla who wanted to dry out—and Gerald would return the favor.

In the days immediately after Cali's body was found crumpled at the bottom of the subway stairwell, reporters began to show up at Sanctuary. One, accompanied by a photographer, had interviewed Thea and Keren and asked to be shown around the building outside, so they could get some pictures. Gerald and Priscilla were lurking in the parkette next door. They made a beeline for the nurses when they appeared and, brushing the reporters aside, made an unexpected plea: "You have to get us out of here. You have to get us out of here *now.*"

Recognizing that critical moment, the two women handed the reporters off to other staff members and took the couple inside to the clinic. They were adamant, determined, and very much on edge. Priscilla was also four-and-a-half months pregnant. Together, the four of them began to discuss what the next moves might be.

Going to stay with Gerald's mother at her home in another city a six-hour bus ride north of Toronto was the first option. It was the first time she'd heard from her son in years. She had suspected but wasn't sure that he had been homeless; she learned for the first time that she already had one grandchild and would soon have another. She thought long and hard and made a difficult decision: No, they couldn't come stay with her. She was in recovery herself and felt that the three of them together would be such a volatile combination that none of them would have a decent chance at sobriety.

She'd try Gerald's uncle, though. The phone calls flew back and forth. The uncle couldn't take them in either, but he would meet them at the bus station and take them to a coed shelter at which he had some connections. And he'd give Gerald a job, as long as he stayed sober. The nurses tracked down an aboriginal addictions agency that ran a program for pregnant women, wrote the number down, and made sure Priscilla put the paper in her pocket.

More phone calls: Priscilla's aunt, in the west end of the city, would take them in for a couple of nights while they got their stuff together, so that they could get out of the downtown zone that suddenly felt so dangerous to them.

Wayne, who along with Steve Hunter runs Mustard Tree, Sanctuary's work-training program, received a phone call later that evening: Priscilla and Gerald needed a ride out to her aunt's place in the west end. Could Wayne oblige?

When he picked them up, they were querulous and half-drunk.

They wouldn't give him an address but directed him street by street until he got close.

"You can drop us off here," Priscilla said, as if she didn't want him to know where they were actually going. It suddenly occurred to Wayne that he didn't know (he hadn't been told) if the aunt even knew they were coming. If she did, would she receive them in this condition? Did they even intend to stay with the aunt, or were they already getting cold feet and simply looking for a way to slip back into the night?

"Wait here," Priscilla directed and, clambering out of Wayne's van, disappeared around the corner. She returned in a matter of minutes; her aunt was in, and they were welcome. Wayne breathed a sigh of relief. As Gerald got out, Wayne mentioned to them that Mustard Tree was only a few blocks away. If they were looking for something to occupy their time the next day, they could come by for a visit and stay for lunch with the crew. They were noncommittal. *It seemed unlikely*, he thought as he pulled away from the curb, that they would show up.

They appeared midmorning, looking hungover and sounding cranky. They were pretty edgy at first, but as Wayne, Steve, and the program participants showed them around the woodworking shop and the art studio, they began to display a flicker of interest. Going north was a desperation move; they didn't know how long they would be there, but if they came back anytime soon, they could see themselves getting involved at Mustard Tree. Priscilla was drawn to the woodworking and Gerald to the art; it was the first time any of us had seen them show an interest or vision for themselves—the hope of a fruitful life—that ran beyond the drive for mere survival.

Although their stomachs were obviously a little uncertain, they sat down for lunch with the group and ate a little soup. Then Wayne offered to take them to the secondhand shop at the end of the street and buy them a few things so they'd have more than what they were wearing to take north with them.

As they strolled back the way they had come that morning, Wayne noticed splotches of vomit drying on the sidewalk at regular intervals. He said nothing, but by the time they reached the store, they had stopped a few times for Priscilla to freshen up.

It made him nervous anytime Priscilla was out of sight in the store, particularly when she slipped into the women's change room. But she and Gerald actually began to enjoy themselves a little as they searched the racks. Wayne found a pair of jeans with the "Indian" logo of the vintage motorcycle company on them. He wondered to himself, *Can a white guy do this?*

He shrugged to himself and tossed them at Gerald, saying, "Here, I think these are for you."

Gerald looked at them and laughed. They fit, and he happily added them to his pile.

The next morning, Doug Johnson Hatlem picked them up at Priscilla's aunt's place and took them to the depot. Doug's three-year-old daughter, Johanna, drew a picture on the way and gave it to Priscilla as she boarded the bus.

There were so many things that could have gone wrong, so many places where they could have given in to their fear of this new and difficult path, bailed out, and gone back to the street. The efforts of our staff members to help them make this unimaginable transition (literally unimaginable; after ten years on the street, it's doubtful they could truly conceive of what this new life would look like) were exemplary, given the fact that the staff were also in the midst of dealing with the emotional fallout from Cali's murder—their own and that of the rest of the community.

But really, what we were able to offer was ad hoc and pretty ramshackle at best. I don't suppose we truly believed that Priscilla would make that phone call on her own, get into the addictions program, and stick with it. Nor did we expect that Gerald, after years of living moment by moment by his fists and wits on the street, numbing himself with mouthwash and whatever other painkillers he could get his hands on, would be able to sober up and put in week after full workweek with his uncle's roofing company.

Probably the best we hoped for, if we were being honest with ourselves, was that they'd get a rest from their destructive habits, that the people they left behind on our streets would get a reprieve from them, and that the little one on the way would escape fetal alcohol syndrome.

I doubt any of us had the courage to imagine that both of them would stay clean and sober from the moment they stepped onto the bus, or that Priscilla would pass every random urine test, and the two of them would jump through every hoop supplied by the Children's Aid Society, or that several members of our staff would enjoy visits with the proud parents in their own clean, neat apartment.

Lyf, who at the time Priscilla and Gerald were negotiating their escape was immersed in trying to stay close to Brian, Leila, and Seven, marveled at the change he saw when he visited the couple he had only known before as a particularly nasty tag team on the street. Priscilla was sterilizing baby bottles in a pot on the stove when he arrived, watching them carefully to make sure they boiled, but didn't melt. Gerald, he told me, was hilarious with his little boy—tender, besotted, beaming. On the fridge door, secured by a magnet, was Johanna's drawing.

Gerald went straight to work for his uncle and never did get into a treatment program. He does attend some twelve-step meetings. What keeps him sober most of all, he says, is being busy. And having hope.

$ $ $

The great hope of Christian faith is of resurrection to a perfect, endless life. Even the miracle experienced by Lazarus was, in the final analysis, a temporary fix. Years later, he and his sisters must all have faced death again. I've always wondered what the three of them would have said if they'd been asked, after the fact, whether or not it was worth going through the pain, sorrow, and fear of death to experience such an incredible thing.

"Well, death is inevitable, you know," they might have responded gently—*where do these simpletons come up with such questions?* "Lazarus was going to die at some point, or maybe Mary or Martha first. Nothing unique about that; it was inescapable, necessary, and so was our grief. But his resurrection—ah! Now *that* was something glorious, something to fire our hearts with hope to the end of our days!"

If Lazarus' resurrection was only a shadow of the true one to come, so too the end of my life will be the culmination of many small deaths along the way. I knew so much when I was twenty; almost thirty years later, I know so much less. Many specific dreams for my future have died; relationships have gone by the board; opinions once stoutly defended have been abandoned; my body is not what it once was.

Some of those changes I have welcomed; others I have fought as fiercely as I know how, sometimes consciously and sometimes not. In the darkest times of my life, I have heard the voice of the only One who can raise the dead, saying, "There is much in you that must die. Take up your cross and follow me—it will be painful, perhaps even humiliating, but there is a new life for you on ahead. Trust me. I've been down this road before."

We would not have chosen to lose California. We still grieve her passing and ache over the manner of it. If it were in our power, we would have her back, and surely we would treasure her all the more. But resurrection of any kind is not within our power. We can only trust that it is coming, look for it, and embrace it when it arrives.

The Sanctuary staffers—we who are rich[1] and so, some of our friends assume, impervious—battle so often with the sense that we are being swamped by need, grief, anger, unholy hungers, brokenness of every kind—all the things that may be summed up in the deadly little word *sin*. Our own and that of others. We are learning of necessity to die to our own egos, particularly as it regards our ridiculous hope that we might actually save ourselves or another human being, and to rest instead in recognizing and rejoicing in the mysterious, godly new life that sprouts in such surprising places. We are learning that we cannot continue to wallow in death if we hope to attain to the resurrection that is being held out to us.

We continue to rehearse the victories as we began to that night shortly after Cali died. Sometimes we forget for long stretches, losing ourselves in cynicism or self-pity, and are only driven to it again by the rising fear that darkness will overwhelm us. When we stop and look back along the path we have been treading, we see that the glow is not only on the horizon for which we are headed, but that the same source lit the shadows through which we have already been more brightly than we had noticed at the time.

Even writing this book has been such an exercise for me. I am mistrustful of anyone who prattles on about "Victory in Jesus!" As far as I can tell, he never promised to rescue us from trouble or suffering in this life, but only to lead us through it. "Victory" theology—the kind of teaching that suggests things will turn out all right if you just have enough faith—is weak, shallow, and just plain wrong. Our Sanctuary context is so rife with failure, often in the most crushing, humiliating, or even lethal terms, that I would consider it a form of lying to tell a bunch of "success" stories.

But looking back now over what I have written, I realize that most of these stories, from the very first tale about Arthur coming home to "die" to this last one about the new life that grew in Priscilla and Gerald because of Cali's death, bear witness to some greater or lesser degree to the power of resurrection.

Our friends who struggle with so many forms of poverty are the ones who, by the very extremity of their experience, actually guide us— the staff and other "wealthy" members of the community. They lead us away from either a morbid fixation with or paralyzing fear of the many deaths we must die and toward the One who described himself quietly to Martha as "the resurrection and the life" (John 11:25).

Perhaps the greatest poverty among the people who are materially poor in our community is a poverty of imagination. "Where there is no vision, the people perish" (Prov. 29:18 KJV); when people are so bankrupt of hope that they cannot imagine a fruitful, joyful future for themselves, they willingly embrace the things they know will eventually destroy them. Our responsibility, as guides for such companions, who can imagine for themselves only a bitter, lonely death, is to hold the hope of new life—a life that can take root even in the shadow of death—for them and continually guide them toward its source.

Just a few weeks after the birth, Thea showed pictures of Gerald and Priscilla's baby to an older aboriginal woman who is also a member of our community. She has had a hard life, homeless much of the time, and suffering through a series of toxic relationships with men who are addicted and abusive. She pored over the photos.

"Oh, oh!" she exclaimed. "He's so beautiful. Now I have hope again."

The resurrection of one is a gift to many others. We do not, cannot walk alone.

CHAPTER 15

ARRIVAL

So instead of getting to Heaven, at last—
I'm going, all along.
—Emily Dickinson

Not that I have already obtained all this.
—Paul, Philippians 3:12

Many years ago, shortly after the initial street outreach work and the efforts of the band, Red Rain, had led to the beginning of weekly communal worship gatherings at Sanctuary, I spoke to that little group one Sunday evening about Paul's letter to the Ephesian church. There were only, perhaps, twenty of us. Most were wealthy people like me, but about a third were people from the street. It was telling that us middle-class folks struggled to accept that we were, in fact, a "church"—the very word seemed to us to require a more pristine environment, a more structured and predictable "service," and a congregation that did not lean quite so heavily on the presence and participation of people who were dirty, ragged, sometimes foulmouthed, tattooed, and still such public sinners.

We were still just learning that there is no "us" and "them"; there is only "us." They, on the other hand, had no qualms about it at all. They already knew that being a church is all about hanging out together because we're all hungry for God.

The passage under consideration was Ephesians 2:11–22, and I knew that the obvious application of it might present some challenges. I felt that the key concept was expressed in verse 14: "He himself [Jesus] is our peace, who has made the two one and has destroyed the barrier, the dividing wall of hostility."

Paul is speaking of the cultural and religious divide between Jews, who even as Christians thought of themselves as the "chosen people" and of all other ethnicities as second-class citizens, and Gentiles, who thought the Jews were spiritual snobs. The "wall" he refers to is probably an allusion to the one that separated the Court of the Gentiles from the interior of the great temple in Jerusalem. Gentiles were not allowed past that wall; only Jews could move farther in and closer to the place were God was said to dwell.

To state so baldly that God viewed Jews and Gentiles equally as "members of God's household" (v. 19) was a radical notion at the time.

"We don't have this Jew-versus-Gentile problem here," I said that night. "But there is another wall that divides us. It's called money. Some of us here have more than we need, and others don't have nearly enough. Some of us will leave this gathering tonight and return to our own homes, warm beds, closets full of clothing, and cupboards and refrigerators full of food. Some will walk out those doors and find a doorway to huddle in for the night.

"But Paul teaches us that Jesus has broken down the walls that separate people. He is telling us that, because of what Jesus did on the cross, we here—those who have lots and those who have nothing—are

one people, brothers and sisters in Christ. He is calling us to find a way
to live our lives together."

I knew that it cost me very little to say those fine-sounding words.
I could tell that the other wealthy people listening recognized it too;
they went suddenly motionless, wondering how the poor people present would take it. People who are poor are usually powerless; they are
forced to passively accept the effects in their lives of whatever devolves
from the decisions made by people who are rich and influential.

This, however, was a stunning reversal. It was instantly evident
that, really, the poor people in our gathering had the greatest authority
to say "yes" or "no" to this concept. It would cost them so much more
to agree, to embrace the rest of us freely as brothers and sisters, and
to release us to return to our comfortable homes while they shivered
through another long winter night.

I left a long pause and looked with some trepidation from face to
face. As I did so, sliding past the rigid forms of the wealthy ones, I saw,
one after another, the heads of our poorest brothers and sisters begin
to nod in agreement.

"Yes," they were saying. "We are brothers and sisters in Jesus, one
body, and we will not support or build anew a wall of resentment or
expectation between us."

I have so often, in the intervening years, been astonished and hum-
bled by the grace extended to me by my brothers and sisters who have
so little.

In fact, in putting to paper the stories in this book, I have at
times felt like a version of Dennis Moore, the old Monty Python
character—a confused eighteenth-century highwayman who robbed
from the poor and gave to the rich. The stories of my "poor" friends

herein are so much more costly, tragic, and potentially humiliating to tell, and yet they have offered them with such generosity and grace to "rich" people like me (and probably like you, dear reader; there aren't many like Dave, Sheldon, or Mandy who will get their hands on this book), whose struggles they might justifiably dismiss with a contemptuous wave of the hand: "Pain? You don't *know* pain!"

Around the same time period that I gave that talk ("sermon" seems too grand a term for musing out loud before a small group in a dim church basement), I arrived home at about three one winter morning. It wasn't unusual in those days; I had been doing street outreach, and people were often most active late at night. The house was silent. I walked from room to room, spending a minute or two watching each of my children sleep and praying over them. Then I stood at the window of my bedroom and watched the snow blowing drifts across the front yard and into the street.

I thought of those of my friends who were by now hunkering down wherever they could find a little shelter and wondered why it had to be so for them. Before long, I found myself weeping and wondering what I had ever done to deserve all the good things I had. Why had I escaped the horrific abuses many of them had endured? And why, having had such a privileged childhood, did I now enjoy such a secure, protected adulthood, while in their lives, tragedy attracted more tragedy in a seemingly unending chain?

I wrestled with those questions for a long time. There is no real answer for them, no more than there is to "why suffering?" The real question is, "Given that I have landed, through no good or ill of my own, among this tiny and most privileged fraction of people in the world, what will I do about it?"

God, I believe, has granted me resources of intelligence, health, money, emotional stability, position, citizenship, and much, much more in the expectation that I will use those resources to lift up my brothers and sisters who are depressed, set free those who are oppressed, seek healing for those who are afflicted, and share with those who are destitute.

The reversal of the usual power dynamic that evening in the church basement is a case of the exception proving the rule: People who are poor and excluded don't usually get to make choices about who they will interact with or in what circumstances. That's why the Bible doesn't waste time encouraging people who are oppressed to ask their oppressors to please release them or those who are destitute to do a little fund-raising.

God does command, over and over, those who are rich and powerful—the 1 or 2 percent of the world's population that includes the majority of us living in first world nations—to engage with and care for our poorest "neighbors" spiritually, materially, emotionally, and politically. So clear and consistent is this message, so redolent with it is the life and teaching of Jesus, that it must be said: *A wealthy person who claims to follow Jesus and does not find some way to share his or her life and material goods with people who are poor has stumbled off the Way.*

We who are wealthy *must* take the initiative in this. The barriers created by our material advantages preclude people who are poor from almost any opportunity of doing so. What we will discover, as those barriers are destroyed, is that the eternal life Jesus proclaimed flourishes best when people who are rich and people who are poor commit themselves to each other. The immediate, earthly benefit of the personal salvation in which we rejoice is progressively unveiled when we engage in intimate, mutually supportive relationship with each other and so discover that we "are being built together to become a dwelling in which God lives by his Spirit" (Eph. 2:22).

If our church buildings are located in neighborhoods where there are no poor people, perhaps we are attending the wrong churches, or maybe the churches are in the wrong places. Often, we simply have not looked carefully enough: In a first world culture where people who are poor are vilified and the victims of poverty are often blamed for having created their own poverty, they have (not surprisingly) learned to camouflage themselves.

The challenge for the first world church in the twenty-first century is to radically reform itself, such that people who are poor are not merely the subject of outreach efforts, but are found right at the heart of our worshipping communities. Sadly, a great many churches have not even got to the point of doing the outreach. They're too busy trying to figure out how to develop a more relevant and attractive worship style. Short-term mission trips don't really accomplish what we are talking about here. In most instances, the mission team benefits far more than the host community from such visits, and the visitors jet away, having had precious little direct contact with the locals.[1]

These are not easy things to say, and they are much harder to do. We may need to make decisions, as individuals and as communities of faith, that alter in a substantial way the fashion in which we now live. It may mean humbling ourselves to admit that we have mistaken or ignored much of the gospel that Jesus and his followers preached. It will certainly mean coming to grips in a practical way with the truth that all we have belongs to God.

To look down the road and try to imagine where such a course might take us may seem overwhelming. But, as Lao-tzu, Chinese sage of ancient times, is reported to have said, "A journey of a thousand miles begins with a single step." What will your first step be?

The conceit of first, second, and third "legs of the journey" is, I freely admit, shallow, inadequate, perhaps in some ways misleading. This journey is not linear, a mere mechanical progression from point to fixed point until I round the last bend and arrive at a time and place long since calculated.

Like the children of Israel in the wilderness, my path twists and turns, folding back on itself, approaching the same points over and over but from different angles, even after I have set eyes on the land itself. I will not ever—in this life at least—perfectly arrive. On the other hand, every single step, no matter how small, provided only that it is toward God rather than away from him, brings me closer home in some fashion.

Given that this book is about a journey that is far from over, it hardly seemed appropriate to call this chapter a "conclusion."

But perhaps, in a mysterious shadow-of-the-true way, I am in some sense there already. Every step claims some new corner of the Father's house; with every step the house grows more spacious, more brightly lit.

APPENDIX

Note: The following sections come from online blogs posted at www.drewmarshall.ca. Taylor and Sabrina posted them after visiting Sanctuary with Drew Marshall. They have been reproduced with the permission of the authors and edited slightly to address the small errors of grammar, spelling, and format that are common to the extemporaneous nature of blogs and to obscure the identity of churches or organizations other than Sanctuary to which they refer. No other content has been changed.

FROM THE GIGGLE SHACK TO THE APOLLO IN ONE WEEK

BY TAYLOR

Preface

Following our outrageous adventure at the T—, Drew decided to tone down the pomp and circumstance while turning up the fabulousness. The church we went to this week was called Sanctuary and is located right downtown in Toronto at Charles and Church streets, and as everyone in the downtown core knows, there was something quite colorful going on last Sunday. There was no chance of not being noticed this week, so Drew had told us to show up a half an hour prior to the service so that we could take a tour of the church and meet several of its important members. The city was a zoo and parking was terrible, so I ended up parking several blocks away and walking through the bonanza that was Church Street.

I thought going to church in this area on that day was rather funny, as we would be the only people wearing pants for a good six-block radius. On my walk I enjoyed the sights and sounds as there is nothing like tens of thousands of people living care free if only for one afternoon. I walked up to the church, an old redbrick building with a ton of character. As I walked up to Drew, who was sitting on the stairs out front, a couple of tourists, not knowing what the building was, stopped to take a picture of themselves with the brightly colored, artistically done sign hanging on the wall facing the street. I was intrigued; I knew I was in for something different, and after last week I was a little nervous.

Speak softly and carry a loud shirt

Once the three of us had assembled, we entered the building and went up a flight of stairs past an older man holding a straw hat. My fear had left me; there was a calm sense of wonder now. We met the pastor first. He was wearing an eccentric yellow Hawaiian shirt with the usual brightly colored flowers. He spoke very calmly in a quiet voice that exuded a wisdom only achieved through many years of heart-wrenching reality. He introduced us to a fellow who looked like he had seen a hard time too many; as it turns out he used to be homeless and had it not been for the Sanctuary who knows where he would be. I could tell then and there we had found what this experiment was set out to accomplish, a church that saw past the money, power, and the heightened sense of moral superiority that we have grown accustomed to. Charity, real charity. About time.

We then took a tour of the place, starting with my personal favorite, the medical clinic. There was a small doctor's office full with all the fixings, two nurses on staff, and a volunteer doctor. [There are] a great number of patients each week that would otherwise never see treatment. In the corner of the office sat an old wooden rocking chair; we were told it was there for the women because they feel more at home. Home would be the key theme throughout our tour, as they had made an extra effort to give a warm welcoming feeling to the church. The bathrooms had wooden stalls as opposed to the cold, gloomy aluminum ones found throughout this cold expanse. There was a massive kitchen warmly painted where they prepare several free meals a week for the disenfranchised and impoverished. But here is where it truly gets interesting: Not only do they serve meals, but they encourage people to help prepare the meals as well; there is a massive island in the center of the kitchen that could accommodate a dozen people working comfortably. Not only do the individuals get a nice hot meal; they enjoy a social environment and a sense of accomplishment. That is nothing short of powerfully moving.

Next we enter into the large common room that serves many purposes, but mostly just as a comfy place to hang out. At one end of the room is some old beat-up furniture that could probably tell you a few stories. They sat facing a small fireplace, which once again gave a homey feeling. At the other end of the room was a great sliding door that gave way to a fair-sized closet full of clothing that could be taken if need be by those who stopped in for a visit. Once again I was floored; for close to a month now I have been told of all the wonderful things the Christian church provides without any physical evidence of its truth, but here it is, in the flesh. I have to smile: We have traveled to the city's massive churches where thousands worship, and yet we find what we are looking for in a turnout of thirty-five on Sunday. We were also told of a second building where the church owns a woodworking shop so that they can teach useful skills in order to employ some of its followers.

Look out, Carson Daly, Jesus has a request show too

It was time for the service, so we went back upstairs and took our seats. There were roughly thirty-five people at the service; we were told numbers were down this week because of the festivities, but a good turnout was around fifty. The chairs were set up in two lines along the length of each wall and slightly curved to create an ovoid bull's-eye kind of arrangement. At the center sat a table with a loaf of bread and some wine sitting on a wooden handcrafted serving tray. At the one end sat the band headed by the pastor on the keyboard, a couple of young bucks playing guitar and the electric violin. At the back was a gentleman playing a bongo drum. They started the service with music, which has been the norm, but that's where the similarities ended. The music was brilliant; they had a hymnbook packed with great tunes and old favorites, many of which were written by people at the church and bore its name in the copyright information at the bottom of the page. The music was more bluesy jazz than it was gospel, and that suited me just fine. We had found out that unfortunately the majority of the band was away that day and we were missing out. The old organ, which formerly sat on stage at the famous Apollo Theatre, stood silent at the back of the room under a sheet. I thought the whole religious relics thing was a more Catholic practice, but I would make a pilgrimage to hear that old thing played. Each person was given a hymnal, and the music was done by request, which I thought was a great touch.

After the music came a time of silence and personal reflection/worship. Finally a church that doesn't ram their ideas about God down your throat. After about five minutes of silence, a middle-aged man sitting against the far wall pipes up with a prayer. He speaks slowly, and you can see the wheels turning in his mind; he spoke well and I was impressed. Following him a woman read a verse from her Bible that she found appropriate for the occasion. One by one almost everyone in the room began to say a prayer when it was their turn, usually followed by a song request, which was then played. Finally after about forty-five minutes of intermittently broken silence, a handicapped man in the corner had his turn and spoke commandingly; he then spontaneously led the group into Communion.

We took a short break and were back for the sermon portion of the service. It was short and about Paul once again, much to Sabrina's chagrin. He kept it short and very colloquial, which I think better illustrated his points, especially considering his audience. Like I just said, Sabrina found a couple of misgivings within the sermon, but I have to disagree with her; everyone takes creative license with Scripture, and although this time it was obvious, it was done out of obviously good intentions, and therefore I felt it was a good thing to do.

This place was great. Finally a place that understood the *personal* relationship with God that is so important, especially as we move into the future where Sunday service might become a thing of the past. This place gets it; there was no collection plate that I ever saw, and what they gave back to the community could not be measured. There aren't enough good things to say about this place.

There's the quick version of my thoughts. This week has been crazy busy for me at work, so I hope to excuse this somewhat hurried entry. I will try and write more later and look forward to hearing all of your questions and comments.

Cheers,
Taylor

BY GEORGE, I THINK THEY'VE GOT IT!

BY SABRINA

This past Sunday was the end of Pride Week in Toronto, and so, really, what better time to go down to a church on Charles Street? Aside from the inevitably crazy traffic and crowded subways, I couldn't wait to see how a Christian church managed itself in the heart of the biggest gay/les/bi/trans festival in the country!

The service was being held at 5:00 p.m., but we went down at about 4:30 so we could see the place properly. This is the one time Drew gave the church the heads-up that we were on our way, and I'm grateful. Not only was it such a small service that we would clearly have been "outed," but we had the chance to speak to Greg Paul, the executive director at Sanctuary, and talk about what they do there.

We were introduced to a man in the most awesome Hawaiian shirt I've ever seen, who had a calm and friendly demeanor about him. When Drew ribbed him a little about the shirt, he told us about the "loud shirt competition" on Sundays. In fact, as I looked around at the gathering congregation, I saw that people were wearing what-ever they felt like! I suddenly felt much less guilty for wearing my flip-flops to church. And that, really, is the beginning of understanding how different this place is.

I was most impressed when he said, by way of introduction, "We believe it's important to do things the way that Jesus actually did. Jesus gave the good news to the poor first; that's where we start."

Sanctuary is a church—but also an outreach center to women, the homeless, alcohol and drug addicts, a vibrant community, an employment center, a small medical office, an art/music/drama program, a support group, and much, much more. In the words of Greg, "We consider everything that we do out of this building to be 'church.' And the people that come here, they may not describe it as being in a church setting, but that's how we see it."

I can't tell you how absolutely refreshing it was to hear those words. I knew I was in for a rare vision—real Christians in action. I wasn't wrong!

And so, on with the review!

The Church: Sanctuary (www.sanctuarytoronto.ca)

Denomination: For once, I didn't get a sense that they were of a particular denomination. I neglected to ask what they call themselves. But my impression was that they were "merely Christian," in the words of the great C. S. Lewis—that is to say, not so focused on the outward appearance of their beliefs, but on how they actually behave.

The Area: Right downtown Toronto, Yonge Street, south of Bloor.

The Building: A building that looked more like what people think of when you say "church"—older looking, brownish brick, steeple up top. Immediately inside were the wooden stairs I remembered from my childhood.

Walking into the sanctuary, you see a big room with chairs in a circle, with a keyboard and guitar set up at the base of the circle. In the center of the circle of chairs was an altar made of wood—looked like it was hand-carved—with "In Remembrance of Me" carved into one side. On top of this were a loaf of bread and a cup of wine with several little mini-serving cups! As someone who has endured the horror of sharing a cup of sacred wine during cold season, I couldn't get over the simple brilliance of this!

Opposite the keyboard (at the "twelve o'clock," if you will) was a simply made wooden cross draped with a red cross. There was a tremendous amount of power in the simplicity of the symbolism.

Did you ever see *Indiana Jones and the Last Crusade*? There's that scene near the end where Indy is faced with choosing, out of many different cups, the one that is the Holy Grail. He's looking carefully, and amid all the gold and silver and gleam, he picks out a simple cup that really would have befitted a pauper. And of course, that's the cup of Christ. The metaphor is obvious, right? Jesus was a guy who valued simplicity, because keeping things simple means you can focus on what you're doing—in his case, "being there" for the outcasts of the world.

This place is like the cup that Indy chose. Amid all the pomp and circumstance of the Christian world out there, here lies a simple, honest place that really means it.

On a brief tour of the building before the service, we were shown the infirmary—where two nurses and many volunteer medical staff serve as community health providers and caregivers. They are familiar faces in a sea of health workers who are all too likely to judge and demean the homeless or working poor—the kinds of people who feel that Sanctuary is like a home. We were shown the drop-in kitchen— where those eating the food actually get together and make it! A gorgeous kitchen that, despite the necessary stainless steel, looked very homey and cozy.

Greg talked about how making meals together builds a sense of community and also how making your meals will often have the effect of changing your view of yourself. Instead of someone who is receiving charity, you're now someone who's taking part in making a meal. Same thing with the creative programs, the art initiatives that make a person go from thinking they're nothing to thinking, *Hey, I've got something to give this world!*

And he's absolutely right—the small perspective changes are what make all the difference to a person's life. It's what makes them able to see a future for themselves. Tell that to the people who marketed *The Secret*, eh? ☺

We were shown the big open room in the basement that sometimes gets used for arts programs, sometimes for drop-in lunches, sometimes just as community space. We saw a roomful of donated clothes for people who need them. We were told about shower facilities and places where people could stay if they needed to. Greg mentioned briefly their employment skills programs before leading us back upstairs for the service. Basically, his overview was to show us that they take their role as Christians seriously—the job is to model their giving on the way that Christ gave. TJ and I were both delighted by what we'd seen so far.

The People: A wide variety! Greg admitted that his congregation was approximately halved because of the Pride festivities that day. There was a young woman visiting from New Zealand, an older woman who recognized Drew and actually knew TJ and me (!), a man in a wheelchair who was dancing appreciatively to the fabulous music, one woman who was signing the songs she was also singing, and many more. What's more, the community seemed really tight—there was a lot of greeting and hugging and happiness.

What I really sensed from every congregant was an immense honesty. The entire service was very heartfelt, which was very touching.

The Preacher: As I indicated, a very friendly guy with not a trace of arrogance in him. The delivery of the "service" was possibly the most enjoyable part of the experience.

Greg started by calling people to attention and talking about the meaning behind the bread and the wine. He talked about how taking Communion was very important symbolically and how it was important to know what it meant before you did it. He started things off by playing the first song: "People Get Ready," one of my faves! Greg is really talented and he clearly loves music. There were also a guitarist, a drummer, and a man playing an electric violin.

We soon noticed the songbooks on the seats around us. We grabbed one and flipped through it. The next song was called out by a member of the congregation: "I think today would be a great day to do number twenty-one," which was a song about how everybody is welcome in God's house. In fact, every song was called out by the congregation. The music ranged from traditionals (like the "theme song" of our journeys, "How Great Thou Art") to music by Van Morrison, to originals by "Sanctuary Music."

I said to Taylor at one point, "Do you see how all the power in this ceremony is coming from the people and not the preacher?" It was beautiful.

There was a point at which Greg asked everyone to sit quietly for a bit, and if anyone wanted to share a passage or a prayer, they were welcome to. There was some quiet, and then one member of the community opened up in a truly heartfelt prayer. I was stunned, not only by the touching honesty but by the reception—most people, in the face of that kind of honesty, shrivel up and hide. Most people cannot face another person spilling their soul, and even fewer can do it in public. Such were the strength and the supportive nature of this group.

A few others read passages that had obviously touched them recently. The group went through a few more songs, and then another man went into prayer. This was the man who danced in his wheelchair, and his speech was clear but halting. I looked around for the telltale signs of impatience and saw absolutely none. This man spoke from his heart, and he went up to the altar and took the first Communion—effectively leading the group to take Communion. I found it inspiring to see the people leading the ceremony, and not being asked to sit still and be preached at.

Then, after some more songs, the group took a short break—enjoyed cornbread and juice—and then sat for a bit of Bible study. The passage in question was Paul's letters to the Galatians—chapter 6, I think. The greatest thing about the delivery was that Greg would read the passage and then close the Bible and say, "OK, this is what that meant."

He talked about the need for Christians to accept that it was an either-or proposition—if you accept that Christ is the Son of God, you must "die to everything else." But he talked about how this gives you a sense of freedom—and how do you use that freedom? To be involved in caring for your brothers and sisters. True freedom comes from loving one another. Bear one another's burdens, and make efforts not to make others responsible for you. He talked about the importance of love and care and of doing it rather than boasting about it—as in verse 14, "Far be it from me to boast the acceptance of the cross."

Would that more Christians practiced this way! There was a very strong sense of interpreting the message for the crowd and preaching it as a message of liberation. What a great thing to see.

The Tunes: As I've said, fabulous, and absolutely intrinsic to the service. Nobody was forced to stand up and sing—people did if they wanted to; they sat if they wanted to. People called out the ones they wanted or needed to hear that day. It was a creative, holistic service. And Greg's little group there has some consummate skill!

Summary Comment: Really, really inspiring—not only because of all of the good works their community is doing, but also because they are real Christians walking the talk. Suffice to say that I've found the place that will be receiving my clothing donations now that I'm moving into the city. These people are the schnazz—and what's great is, they don't have any of the spiritual arrogance that drives me nuts.

NOTES

Chapter 1

1. Throughout this book, names and identifying details of both the persons and their stories mentioned have generally, though not always, been changed to protect the privacy and dignity of my friends—both those who are "rich" and those who are "poor."

Chapter 2

1. A wildly out-of-context quote from Mark 14:7. Jesus was himself quoting Deuteronomy 15, where God starts off by saying, "If you do what I tell you, there will be no poor among you," and ends with the sad conclusion, "There will always be poor among you" because of his people's disobedience and greed. Jesus' audience would have recognized the quote immediately and realized that he was tacitly criticizing their hypocritical "concern" for the poor.

Chapter 3

1. "Boystown," *Eye of the Hurricane*, Sanctuary Records © 1995. This and other Red Rain CDs are available at www.sanctuarytoronto.ca.

Chapter 4

1. A radical oversimplification, but I'll assume that most readers are as foggy about how the brain actually works as I am. My apologies if you actually understand it....

Chapter 5

1. There is much debate about the actual site of the town in the biblical story, and depending on which version you read, the distance quoted is either this or about seven miles. Check it out on Wikipedia if you want. I've chosen the one favored by most scholars.

2. Henri Nouwen's beautiful and powerful book *The Return of the Prodigal Son* centers around the Rembrandt painting of that name and is one of the reasons I've come to love Rembrandt's work so much. Nouwen's treatment of the painter's life and spiritual journey, as well as the biblical story that particular painting illustrates so profoundly, is much deeper than anything I could attempt.

The First Leg of the Journey

1. Canadian one- and two-dollar coins.

Chapter 6

1. The whole story can be found in *God in the Alley*, by Greg Paul (Colorado Springs: Shaw Books, 2004).

Chapter 7

1. Sabrina and Taylor posted blogs about their visit on Drew's Web site a few days later. You'll find them in the appendix.

2. www.drewmarshall.ca.

3. Not nearly as callous as it sounds. Drew likes to say that a church's success should be gauged by the number of ugly people in it—the more the better. I doubt he intends the word *ugly* to refer only or even primarily to physical appearance.

Chapter 8

1. Marty, Lenny, Frank, and Brian have since passed away—untimely deaths, all. I miss them and remember their friendly laughter with gratitude.

2. I concede that I have not here applied this passage with the most rigorous sense of context.

Chapter 9

1. www.cbc.ca/health/story/2007/09/25/depression-study.html. (Accessed September 25, 2007.)

2. The entire eighty-three-minute film can be watched in chapters at the following permalink:
www.youtube.com/view_play_list?p=FA50FBC214A6CE87.

3. And it must be said that, although corporations are presented here as the primary exemplars of a dysfunctional kind of productivity, many other systems, including the church in its various manifestations, exact a similarly high price from those who participate in them.

Chapter 10

1. No disrespect intended here to my Anglican brothers and sisters or the Anglican (Episcopal) Church. About a third of our staff and board are passionate followers of Jesus in the Anglican tradition.

Chapter 11

1. … and one that, were I to actually write it here, would disqualify this book from sale by members of the Christian Booksellers Association.

2. Romans 8:25.

Chapter 12

1. Geoff is also the editor of *The Rubicon*, an online theological magazine (www.therubicon.org), and the author of several challenging books.

Chapter 14

1. Comparatively, of course. None of our staff members make the kind of incomes they could elsewhere. For the privilege of working in such challenging circumstances, they also agree to raise their own support, as missionaries do.

Chapter 15

1. Habitat for Humanity projects, for instance, do benefit host communities with the construction of much-needed buildings, including homes, and I have supported my own children in going on such trips. There is, however, little opportunity for visiting teams to develop the "companionship on the way" I'm describing with their hosts, given that they are usually only there for one brief stay. I do know some first world churches that have built long-term, meaningful, mutually fruitful relationships with third world communities by making repeated visits to the same place and staying in regular contact. In such circumstances, it's almost inevitable that some of those "wealthy" visitors fall in love with the people and place and end up finding a new home among them.

[SANCTUARY]

View and order products from the Sanctuary community, including CD's by Red Rain, artwork or beautiful one-of-a-kind furniture from our Mustard Tree program.

Music

Sell the Farm...
(Dan Robins)

A Night at Grace's
(Red Rain)

Christmas Songs
(Red Rain)
Available Nov 2008

Art

Furniture

www.sanctuarytoronto.ca/store

[SANCtuaRY] ... A Place of Refuge

At Sanctuary, we are becoming a healthy, welcoming

community where people who are poor or excluded

are particularly valued. This community is an expression

of the good news embodied in Jesus Christ.

SANCTUARY MINISTRIES

25 Charles Street East

Toronto, Ontario M4Y 1R9

Tel.: 416-922-0628

Fax: 416-922-4961

info@sanctuarytoronto.ca

www.sanctuarytoronto.ca